D1474616

THE
SOUL
AND
THE
ETHIC

BY

ANN REE COLTON

ARC PUBLISHING COMPANY
POST OFFICE BOX 1138
GLENDALE, CALIFORNIA 91209

First Edition
Second Printing, 1976

Printed in the United States of America
BOOK GRAPHICS, INC.
Marina del Rey, CA 90291

Dedicated
to all who
would listen to
their Angels

FOREWORD

The soul of man has long remained a mystery. For ages the mystery of the soul has continued to intrigue and to inspire those who contemplate man's relationship with God. Many persons have intuited that the soul is the cherished link between man and his Maker, but few have been able to contribute new truths about the nature of the soul.

The Scriptures often refer to the dangers that beset the soul, the burdens that press heavily against the soul, the sorrows that sadden the soul, and the joys that cause the soul to sing.

For many years Ann Ree Colton has been a *soul singer*—one who has given freedom to her soul's voice through the beauty and inspiration of her spiritual words and creative works. To her, the soul is not a mystery—it is an ever-present reality, a "breathing, animated vortex of light."

She has learned that the soul reflects the ageless record of all that one has experienced from

iv

time immemorial. She sees the soul as a source of hidden riches waiting to be discovered. And most important of all—she tells one how to find the keys to the soul's sacred treasures.

The chapter on "The Medallion of the Soul" describes the author's revelations as to why "the paramount sphere of the soul's action is around the head." The chapter on "Prayer, Contemplation and Meditation" gives exact formulas for liberating the soul's gifts and talents, and for coming closer to the threshold of Heaven. The five contemplative chapters and their accompanying mantrams contain a philosophical, poetic, and revelatory theme. The chapter on "Ethics and Disciplines" enumerates the necessary requirements for activating and sustaining the soul's noblest impulses.

Ann Ree Colton has often spoken to me of her deep desire to write a book about the soul, the spiritual practices, and pure ethics. I share her joy in knowing that *The Soul and the Ethic* has become a reality. I also rejoice with those who will receive from this beautiful book the instruction and the inspiration for which they yearn.

JONATHAN MURRO

ACKNOWLEDGMENTS

I wish to express my gratitude to my devoted associate, Jonathan Murro, for his untiring guidance and assistance. His inspired editing has been a necessary strength supplementing my efforts throughout the years.

I also wish to give thanks for additional editing helps received from my beloved friends, Anastasia Wilson, Alban McRoberts, Serena Burris, and Tobias DeMarchi.

CONTENTS

1   The Medallion of the Soul   1

2   Prayer, Contemplation and Meditation . . .   23

3   Grace   48

4   Conscience and the Soul   89

5   Creation and Healing   123

6   The Initiation of the Heart   151

7   Thought and Will   168

8   The Spiritual Life   199

9   Ethics and Disciplines   214

   Index   255

To be whole,
To be one,
This is joy.
For the One,
Through whom we move and have our being,
Contains the whole,
The all.
And thus we seek
To know,
To understand,
And to express that which we know.
The Holy Spirit offers us
The cup of cold water,
Quenching our thirst for knowledge.
Let our souls
Become as golden harpsichords
For God,
Singing the song of God,
The Spirit Eternal.

1

THE MEDALLION OF THE SOUL

O men, be not separate;
For all come from the one Source,
And all return to the one Source.
And all is creation.
If the song is sad,
And the foot is weary,
Look thou not back.
But look into the blazing glory of
  thy soul's sun,
And see the light accompanying
  thee.

Good is an imperishable treasure. The immortal record of good is never lost; it survives from life to life, from eternity to eternity. This record and reservoir of good is called *grace*. Faulty actions colored by self-will, or by continued indecisive thinking, will shut one away from his record and reservoir of good. However, it is inevitable that he will benefit, in some future time, from the golden record of his good.

The reservoir of good or grace rests within the *medallion of the soul*. The medallion of the soul is a scintillating sphere of supernatural light penetrating and surrounding the area of

1

the head. The inner portion of this holy light contains the grace one has earned through good works.

Regardless of how laggard a person has been in previous lives or how laggard he may appear in this life, his soul's medallion reflects his reverence for good, his intent of good, and his merciful acts of good. The medallion of his soul enables him to have access to the good and the mercy of the world through which he may receive charitable and loving helps, and be retrieved in moments of trial or need. No person is so completely corrupt, weak or depraved that he cannot be helped—if he will repent, turn toward his good, and believe on the power of good.

The desire to be good, the desire to be thought good, and the desire to be the receiver of goodness and perfection come from an inner knowing of the power of good and from the memory of the expression of good in former lives. However, in each embodiment or life, a person must exert the effort to reinstate his treasures of good. Good may be seen in a person as tenderness, consideration and loving-kindness toward the weak and helpless; in selfless and devoted works for the world; in merciful and compassionate attitudes toward the frailties of mankind. One who has achieved inner goodness is the tender father, the loving mother, the charitable judge, the good steward, the devoted aspirant, the dedicated healer.

The medallion of the soul is filigree-like, in that it consists of countless patterns and hues formed and colored by the former pure actions and good works in innumerable existences or lives in previous eras, ages, and epochs. The medallion of the soul resembles the aurora borealis, for the spiritual atoms of man's physical, emotional, mental, and etheric bodies concentrate and center their reflected light within the medallion of the soul. When a person seeks to live a higher life of dedication, the grace within the medallion is quickened and stirred— and he is inspired to purify his emotions and to illumine his thoughts.

Each small or insignificant act, each deed of greatness, is recorded in some manner or degree upon the medallion of the soul. When there is a preponderance of unresolved or darkened actions from this life or former lives, such darkness seals away and obscures the benefits or rewards of grace. Through sustained spiritual practices, one stills the thunderous roar of unfinished and unresolved acts obstructing his expression of pure feelings and thoughts—so that he may remain in continued rapport with the immortal good within the medallion of his soul. With self-discipline, conscientious effort, and undeviating honesty, one will come, in time, to channel his good or grace to the world, and he will receive the unrestrained freedom of his soul-powers.

The Soul-Powers of Man and the Rhythm of God

The soul has an eloquence which only those obedient to the laws of God can hear, a life-restoring only the faithful may know, a wisdom only the truthful may apply, and a love only the pure in heart may receive. When one imbalances, distorts, or refutes the laws of God, and becomes a law unto himself, he steps away from the Rhythm of God. When he feels himself to be omnipotent, or when he uses his self-will to abuse his fellow man, the results are evil, suffering and sorrow. One suffers because he seeks to remain apart from God rather than to become a part of Him.

Persons who willfully violate the laws of God are incapable of blending with the Rhythm of God—for the resourcefulness and powers of the soul are restrained. Such persons eat the bitter bread of wasted and worthless works. When one is dependent on self alone, he lives in cyclic timing correlating solely to the physical world. When the Rhythm of God is recovered, one may move out of the chaos of distortion, evil, sorrow and suffering. A person who correlates to the Rhythm of God from age to age has access to the higher soul-powers and becomes an anointed server of mankind.

God has given to man, through his soul-powers, an eternal resourcefulness to cope with an eternity world. Through the soul-powers, man may correlate to the Rhythm of God and may be continually regenerated, rejuvenated, revived and restored—for the soul-powers are the imperishable, immortal and undying instruments of communicableness with God. The soul-powers seek to make man more godlike, that he may become a co-creator with God.

> *O men, arise!*
> *Thy world is in thy hands,*
> *Even as the earth is in the Hand of God.*
> *Be at home in thyself.*
> *Thy destiny is of God.*
> *He has willed thee to be.*
> *He has willed thee to become.*
> *Listen to the wonder in thee—*
> *The holy wonder.*

The Medallion and the Soul-Powers

The soul-powers seek to blend the will of man with the Will of God. When one brings his lesser will and sentient nature into obedience, his emotional nature into harmony, and his mental nature into lucidity, the Will of God may work through him. Selfless, dedicated works, sacrifice, the looking within, and facing all issues directly will enable the student of the spiritual life to free the soul-powers and to receive the benefit of his good works from former lives.

To be fascinated and enticed by the will of the lesser self in emotions and thought nullifies the powers of the soul and, therefore, shuts away the Will of God. To deny the Will of God nullifies the powers of the soul and seals away the benefit of good or grace from former lives. When faith is wavering or dimmed, one limits his soul-powers and receives his good from former lives in fragments and parts rather than in a continued and rhythmic action. A skeptical person is unaware of his good and of the manifold blessings in the world around him. Continued doubt, denial, skepticism, lack of faith, and abuse or faulty stewardship of good will seal away, for many lives, the receiving of good. Persons with such qualities may be said to "lose" their souls—that is, to lose touch with the grace aspect of their soul-powers. The continued love of physical possessions rather than the love of God will also separate man from the higher powers of his soul.

> For what is a man profited, if he shall gain the whole world, and lose his own soul? or what shall a man give in exchange for his soul?
> —St. Matthew 16:26

Each person entered this eternity or earth with five soul-powers. These soul-powers cannot be cultivated externally or deliberately developed—for they are perfected. However, the soul-powers may be restrained from their perfect action when a person has been, in this life or in some other life, willfully disobedient to the laws of God. When the will of man and the Will of God work as one, the five soul-powers are unhampered and are free to utilize the highest degree of light from man's eternal or spiritual atoms. In this, the soul-powers stir, stimulate and quicken the various levels of good or grace recorded within the medallion.

The five soul-powers are Vibration, Radiation, Illumination, Emanation, and Pulsation.

Vibration The Vibration power of the soul works through the outer field or rim of the soul's medallion. The Vibration power of the soul, moving against the forces of gravity, creates a *vibratory hum*. The outer rim or vibratory hum collects the energy-filled negations caused by wrong actions, feelings, and thoughts in this life and in other lives. The vibratory hum is the unrelenting reminder of the imbalanced physical actions and debts of this life and former lives— actions and debts which are yet to be defined and resolved. The vibratory hum, in certain stages of man's evolvement, becomes the voice of his conscience. When one refuses to hear the voice of his conscience, the vibratory action of this soul-power irritates the emotions and thoughts, and his higher soul-powers become immobilized. Such persons are materialistic, agnostic, or atheistic—believing only on physical works as their god, or in the physical dollar as their only supply, or in sensual and physical relationships as their only gratification.

To seal away the conscience for a prolonged period of many lives brings one perilously close to an imbalanced mentality and an amoral feeling-world. However, when the voice of conscience is consistently obeyed, the vibratory hum of the medallion is stilled—and one may have access to the levels of grace residing in the filigree light of the medallion.

Some persons live in poisonous thinking-worlds because, over a long period, they have built malice, envy, jealousy, covetousness, lust, greed, deceit; thus, they continually think evil of other men. Such persons are cynical and unbelieving. When one's thoughts are disturbed, depressed, revengeful, or over-aggressive, he accumulates more resisting energies upon the vibratory hum of the soul's medallion. Therefore, it is important that one sustain good will in his feelings toward others, and that he hold charitable thoughts toward those whom he knows—and even toward those unknown to him.

All pure creators live in a world of creative thinking. Such persons are in direct contact with the inner light of their soul's medallion.

Prayer, contemplation, meditation, and the speaking of mantrams cleanse the vibratory hum—and enable one to listen to the guidance of his soul, to free the grace of good works, to receive the blessings from his good, and to express original and creative talents.

The vibratory hum extends to the ears, the sinuses, and the eyes. During the practice of meditation, one may sometimes experience irrelevant thoughts which intrude upon the quieting of his thoughts and the stilling of his senses. This disturbance is caused by the action of the vibratory hum. One should persevere from day to day so as to calm this restless vibrational sea, for as long as a darkened or shaded portion remains within the vibrational field, he will be restrained from the full use of his soul-powers. Therefore, it is the work of the spiritual seeker to set his life into order emotionally and mentally—and adhere, without variance, to the reverent, devotional, and spiritual practices of prayer, contemplation, meditation, and mantramic speaking. This will enable him to clear and cleanse the vibrational field of the soul's medallion. Thus, he will begin to enter more freely into the spiritual areas or fields of his medallion, and thereby release his higher soul-powers to the fullest capacity of their expression.

Negative dreams at night are influenced by the vibratory hum of the soul's medallion. Beautiful, symbolic, instructive dreams are influenced by the pure side of the soul's medallion.

In the center of the forehead resides a spiritual portal called the imaging portal. The higher imagination is active in this portal.

In the center or crown of the head the will is active. When the will is used within the Will of God, the soul's medallion becomes illumined, and the vibratory hum is overpowered by the effulgent light of the soul.

At the base of the skull resides the memory portal. If the vibratory hum is heavy with negation, one remembers fearful things. He lives in a state of bondage, and expresses the spirit of fear. When the soul's medallion is clear and free through purity, the memory is unobstructed and pure.

The subconscious mind is the dark side of memory. The true mentality is a mind fixed on God, in which the imagination, the will, and the memory are united—and the soul's medallion becomes a golden nimbus of radiant light.

Even as the outer portion of the soul's medallion has a vibratory hum which reflects or silhouettes a person's negative and unresolved actions, so is there a vibratory hum around the earth which reflects the unresolved actions of mankind. This vibratory hum around the earth is the *world subconscious.*

The evil deeds of a person, reflected within and upon the vibratory hum of the soul's medallion, correlate to the satanic forces in the world subconscious. A person can be stirred by evil and activated into wrong action when he still retains a residue or portion of evil around the vibratory hum of his soul's medallion.

The love of God, the sustained reverence toward all men, a pure heart, pure intent, and sincere dedication will protect a person from being led into wrong actions instigated and insinuated telepathically from the subtle forces within the world subconscious.

Radiation The Radiation field of the soul's medallion correlates to the pituitary gland and to the line directly above the eyebrows. The soul-power of Radiation works directly with the Love of God through the Radiation field of the medallion. The filigree of the Radiation field records and discloses all works of pure love, reverence, devotion, sacrifice, and renunciation. The Radiation power of the soul makes it possible for one to love selflessly and to sacrifice for love's sake. The soul-power of Radiation, working upon the field of Radiation, endeavors to assure each person of the Love of God. Thus, man always hungers for love and seeks to express love in some degree.

When one is saturated with love for the world, the love for money, or is lustful in his love relatings, he increases the intensity of the vibratory hum—and he is shut away from the Radiation field of love. When one has cleansed his heart, he has an alignment with the Love of God, and radiates a pure, loving presence.

**Illumi-
nation**   The Illumination field of the soul's medallion correlates to the center of the forehead. The Illumination power of the soul works directly with the Light of God and the Light of the Christ through the Illumination field. The Illumination power of the soul makes it possible for a person to work creatively through imaginative thought and to think with uninterrupted inspiration. All creative thoughts and spiritual telepathic symbols are germinated within the Illumination field of the soul's medallion.

Emanation   The Emanation field of the soul's medallion correlates to the hairline of the head. The Emanation power of the soul works directly with the Life of the Father and with the Living and Eternal Spirit of God through the Emanation field of the medallion. The Emanation field contains the record of miraculous works, and enables one to give life to his faith. When there is undeviating faith, the soul-power of Emanation gives to a person the effulgent love of life and the power to draw from within himself a resource of restoring and sustaining life in spite of trial, persecution, or repression. The Emanation power of the soul makes it possible for one to be the receiver of miraculous help or healing in right timing.

Pulsation   The Pulsation field, the brightest point of the soul's medallion, is in the exact center of the top of the skull and correlates to the pineal gland.

The Pulsation power of the soul works directly with the Will of God through the Pulsation field. The Pulsation power of the soul works in tides of ebb and flow. This power of the soul, working with the Rhythm of God, continues relentlessly and persistently to return man to the physical world through rebirth—until the plan of God for man is fulfilled. Regardless of how far a person has removed himself from the plan of God, he shall return, in time, to the original plan in creation for him.

The Pulsation power of the soul correlates to the heartbeat of man. When the heart is a prayerful, loving and devoted heart, the Pulsation power of the soul and the heartbeat become as one. When the heartbeat of man ceases at death, the Pulsation power of his soul becomes the heartbeat of his everlasting body.

THE FIVE SENSES AND THE SOUL-FACULTIES

Thread thy needle, and mend the sore places. Be diligent, but be thou not hypersensitive—that is, be thou not over-tense as to wounds yet open. Know that if thou quickenest the restoring powers, thou shalt receive the anointing; then followeth the natural restoring, and, finally, the healing of the small wounds in the feeling-world.

Good rules fall upon the ears of the

ready. If thou wouldst speak into the ears of men with love, thy words will reach beyond the eardrums, and will return men to purity, to chaste ideals, to noble intent; and more than this, thy words will inspire men to keep holy in their chastity of consecration, and will instill love into selfless hands—hands which hold themselves upward in the Gothic-like arch of that which dedicates.

To teach men to refrain from that which grasps, and which would wrench or force, or which would sculpture out by will, thou shouldst direct their hands to become holy, selfless hands—fused together as healing flames through which the ignition of the Spirit may work with the need in the feeling-world.

Make men feel they are worthy objects. Degrade not any man. Comfort men with the anointing of love. The love of God hath many channels in the Healing Ministry. The love of God must touch the feelings of man. If thou hast not the love of God, thou canst not be a healer of the feelings of man.

In the Edenic or etheric period of the earth— previous to the time when man took a "coat of skin," or a physical body—the senses of man were quiescent, and man used his soul-faculties rather than his senses. As the forces of gravity began to press upon man, his soul-faculties projected, one by one, five lesser degrees of sensitivity—the senses.

The first sense to be oriented to the pressures of gravity was the sense of smell.

> And the Lord God formed man of the dust of the ground, and breathed into his NOSTRILS the breath of life; and man became a living soul.
> —Genesis 2:7

The second sense to be manifested was the sense of touch.

> . . . Ye shall not eat of it, neither shall ye TOUCH it, lest ye die.   —Genesis 3:3

The third sense to experience the gravity world was the sense of taste.

> . . . she took of the fruit thereof, and did EAT, and gave also unto her husband with her; and he did EAT.   —Genesis 3:6

The fourth sense to be activated was the sense of sight.

> And the EYES of them both were opened . . .
> —Genesis 3:7

The fifth and last sense to be quickened was the sense of hearing.

> And they HEARD the voice of the Lord God . . .
> —Genesis 3:8

After the five senses became acclimated to the pressures of gravity, man was prepared to experience life in a physical world.

When man began to use his senses rather than his soul-faculties, the sense of smell gave him the power to discriminate between the pleasant and the unpleasant, the pure and the impure. His sense of touch enabled him to gauge shapes, forms, structures. The sense of taste, working with the chemistry and digestive system of his body, told him when he was hungry or not hungry, and taught him to discriminate between what suited or repelled his palate. The sense of sight enabled him to gauge distance, dimensions, height and depth. He saw the faces of those around him, and he liked or disliked what he saw. The roar of the rivers and the sound of new earth in the making pressed upon the aural cavities of his ears. His hearing warned him when his enemies were in pursuit of him. He heard the music of the birds and learned to differentiate the sounds identifying each living thing.

Henceforth, man used his senses as the instruments through which he discriminated between good and bad on every level of life. However, he would remain for long aeons uncertain as to the higher use of his senses, for in his intensified encasement in the world of sensation, pressed by the need to survive, man's senses became predominantly instinctual rather than spiritual. Gradually, as he evolved, man became aware that he was able to experience a higher aspect of his senses. It has been the work in all ages for teachers, sages, prophets, and saviours to remind man that he is more than his senses—

to remind him that his senses may be extended into soul-faculties.

The soul-faculties are free to act when one trains his feelings, disciplines his desires, and channels his emotions into pure and true expressions of love.

The super-sense, which men throughout the ages have called the "sixth sense," is the result of a united flow between the senses and the soul-faculties.

When the sense of smell is at one with its correlating soul-faculty, it becomes the divining power of intuition, and the power to breathe life into pure forms.

In spiritual experience, the sense of touch keeps one in touch with God, and becomes the power to ascertain life's continuity. The sense of touch enables one to feel with his hands the *etheric braille* of the Higher Worlds, and to be aware of a holy blessing or anointing from heavenly presences. The sense of angelic touch is experienced by the spiritual aspirant when he becomes aware that an angelic presence has touched him and healed him.

The sense of taste, when free within its higher soul-faculty attribute, enables one to partake of the sacred bread of God, to eat at the Lord's table in certain heavenly initiations. In the physical world, when the soul-faculty of taste is used, one receives the power to attain oneness with the substance of God, the power to receive the strengthening manna for his physical body, and the power to receive nourishment during periods of fasting. The soul-faculty of taste provides him with a selective palate—and he practices the hospitality and the true agape of the Lord's table.

When one is free to see with holy vision into greater dimensions of light, he sees beyond the personal or partial, and he will eventually receive the power to look upon the greater archetypes or blueprints of God. He beholds the Plan of God and His finished work.

The soul-faculty of hearing produces obedience to the laws of Nature and to the Laws of God. One hears the differentiated tones of the Holy Ghost telling him to render mercy and justice, to forgive those who have sinned against him, to comply with the living ethic or the rules of life. Through the soul-faculty extension of hearing, one hears the harmonious voices of Spiritual Presences.

> *For those who need vision,*
> *May the eye single come unto them.*
> *For those who need hearing,*
> *May the inner ear open to the World*
>   *of God.*
> *For those who need healing speech,*
> *May love come to their tongues.*
> *For those who would minister,*

May the stigmata of their hands
Be opened,
That they may know the true laying
*   on of the hands*
In Christ Jesus.

In the spiritual life, one learns that the senses are the soul's antennas, and that the soul may speak through reverent senses. When feelings, desires, and love are fulfilled with reverence, the senses are spiritually quickened.

The senses become erratic instruments when one seeks to live through his lower emotional will. This results in a psychic temperament, a manipulative mind. A psychic personality is a fatiguing personality, as uncontrolled psychical power is harmful to those who have little understanding of the dangers in the dark side of mental and manipulative magics.

It is necessary for all dedicated disciples to avoid psychical pitfalls. One should refuse to let his senses dwell upon the chimeras of mysticism. He should qualify—with ethic and with truth—each thing observed through his senses. He should strive to make all things in his world of feeling, emotions, and desires unalterably pure.

When the emotions are morally purified, and the desires wholly at one with the intent of God, the soul-faculties take command of the momentum of emotional expression—and the soul may extend the orbit of its action. When the senses, feelings, and desires blend in equal degree of momentum as to expression, they are similar to the wheels of a moving vehicle, in that they work in unison. Thus, the soul-faculties are freed after a certain coordination is reached by the action of the senses, the feelings, and the desires.

As long as there is an irregularity imbalancing the senses, feelings, and desires, the soul-faculties cannot elucidate to the senses, feelings, and desires what the soul would say. A person who depends completely upon his senses becomes materialistic. One who permits his sensual desires to dominate him becomes a sensualist. But when one's senses, feelings, and desires work in unison with his soul-faculties, he intuits and responds to the Will of God.

Through spiritual aspiration and dedication, the senses become accurate perceivers and recorders; the feelings are clarified, and the desires come into alignment with the true need of the individual. And all things are received by him in their right timing as to his degree of evolvement.

> **But seek ye first the kingdom of God, and his righteousness; and all these things shall be added unto you.**   **—St. Matthew 6:33**

An eternal and inherent soul-fastidiousness in each person seeks to inspire him to purify the senses, the feelings, the desires, and the emotions. Feelings expressed through faulty habits result in unlicensed actions. Undisciplined desires inflict great harm upon others and upon self. If the emotions are channeled through wrong desiring, the result is self-misery and frustration.

In the present age, the majority of persons have either over-aggressive mentalities and immature emotions or over-aggressive emotions and timid mentalities. The person who seeks to live a spiritual life must work to produce pure emotions and an unprejudiced mind. Health of the emotional body is of the uttermost necessity. Emotional maturity can be achieved through (1) right responsibles, (2) self-control, (3) receiving with praise, giving with detachment, (4) love for all life, creatures, persons, (5) continued love phrasings and speakings, (6) love demonstrativeness, (7) love of God and of His creation.

When one is not trained to use love properly, he desecrates love. He is a wastrel of love; and he walks in wastelands, desolate, devoid of the love of God.

Desire is the highest attribute of the emotional body. When one desires to be unfeeling, he becomes a stoic. When he sensually desires to explore and to experiment, he develops a cunning will. When one desires to possess without earning, he short-circuits the natural interflow between soul and emotions. The true desire for selflessness maintains a faultless continuity between the soul and the emotions.

The students and disciples of this age are faced with countless temptations. Each small trial in feeling, desire, and love is but the testing and training so that a perfect emotional body may be formed. Men with perfect emotional bodies, having mastered all gravity temptations, will become the true peacemakers of the earth, and will receive and express hierarchal powers—for the emotional body, when perfected and expressing the highest degree of love, will support and sustain mighty hierarchal ideas directly relating to the Plan of God for this eternity.

There is but a frail barrier between desire and the soul-faculties. Therefore, when desires become qualified as to pure and selfless believing, they will be at one with the soul-faculties. Because desire is closest to the soul-faculties, it is necessary for one to clarify his desire beyond wish or want. Until desire becomes true, and is clarified with lucidity of thought, the result is a chaotic life—and disastrous circumstances are repeated again and again. When men in the earth come to desire selflessly with pure love, they will become harmless to one another and will work as creators for the good of the earth and its creation.

> Therefore I say unto you, What things soever ye desire, when ye pray, believe that ye receive them, and ye shall have them.　　—St. Mark 11:24

2

PRAYER, CONTEMPLATION AND MEDITATION

Pray thou for courage.
And pray thou for strength.
And pray thou for unfailing
*   fortitude.*
And pray thou for wisdom and love.
Pray thou for generosity.
And pray thou for stamina.
And pray thou for forgiveness,
Which doth move on thy tongue in
*   love,*
And which speaketh sharply not to
*   any,*
But speaketh only in the love
*   message*
Of wisdom unto the world.
And pray thou art as wise as a
*   serpent,*
In that thou recognizest evil—
And thou art as gentle as a dove,
Inasmuch as thou holdest the love.

There are as many approaches to prayer as
there are people in the world, for prayer is an
individual action prompted by the conscience
aspect of the soul. However, there are many

precocious personalities in the world today who
have lost the art of praying. Such persons are
casualties of this age of experimentation and
science, and have isolated themselves from the
very essential practice of prayer.

The atheist believes not in God or prayers.
The lethargic, passive and fatalistic person believes that what happens will happen anyway.
The cunning mentalist is convinced that it is
demeaning and humiliating to pray. Filled with
pride, egotism, and a feeling of self-sufficiency,
he depends on his wiles and craftiness to gain
in the world. He gives not of himself, but he
looks on life as the means of acquiring or acqui-
sition. The immature person prays through the
emotional will for self and self alone; he prays
for personal objects and things, and he prays
to be removed from responsibilities placed upon
him. In many persons the compulsion to pray is
motivated by the desire for self-salvation. True
prayer begins when one prays for his fellow
man.

In certain metaphysical schools, the affirma-
tion has replaced prayer. In certain occult
schools, the art of concentration has replaced
prayer. In certain esoteric schools, ritual and
techniques of meditation have taken the place
of prayer. Today, many persons who have experienced training in the metaphysical, the
occult, and the esoteric schools are preparing
to experience the greater rewards of dedicated

discipleship. Thus, they will become ethical propagators of the art of prayer.

> And he spake a parable unto them to this end, that men ought always to pray.
> —St. Luke 18:1

At intervals everyone undergoes a super-scrutiny of his faults. When one dedicates and sincerely desires to correct any uncomeliness in his nature and temperament, he is given the spiritual helps of Heaven. When one faces these cycles of self-scrutiny, and is brought face to face with the mirror of his imperfections, his cumulative prayers become the spiritual power through which he may arise. With continued prayers for improvement and betterment, the mirrored vision of himself becomes more as that envisioned in Heaven.

When many pray together, a voluminous power goes forth into the world. When many contemplate the wondrous ideas of Spirit, the minds of those who are ready in the world are quickened, and they begin to express the golden ideas of the Spirit. When meditation becomes a symphony within perfect timing, correlating to the tides of the Spiritual Worlds, men are raised and lifted. Their burdens become accepted responsibilities; their emotional distractions are converted into humility; and their mental tensions are consumed in the healing fire of the Heavenly Host.

PRAYER AND THE PERSONALITY

Each person has a personality, an individuality or ego, a soul, and a Higher Self. When one is entirely dependent upon his personality, his individuality is but a faint spark—and his Higher Self is totally obscured. When a person is highly evolved, his personality is wholesome and luminous, his individuality is a bright light upon the horizon of mankind, and his Higher Self is apparent, in that all he does has a spiritual portent for the good of the world.

The personality is ennobled and perfected through contemplative thought. The Light of the Higher Self may be experienced through prayer, contemplation, and meditation.

Prayer, contemplation, and meditation are sequential steps in the quest for a spiritual life. When these sacred exercises are observed, one activates a Divine stimulus in his personality and individuality; thus, he begins a spiritual life while living in the physical world.

Prayer is the cleanser and the sweetener of the personality. The conduct of the personality is tempered, softened and made more considerate through prayer. Continued prayer keeps alive the communicableness between the personality and the grace of the soul.

A person who devotes his prayers solely to materialistic wishes or desires short-circuits the grace of his soul and, therefore, nullifies the quality of intuition which would guide and inspire him each day.

When a person absents himself from prayer and communion with God, he is dependent upon the personality alone. Such a person is materialistic and is fearful of life and death, for he shuts himself away from the higher degrees of his soul-grace. He exults in a life of sensuality and personality preservation. He lives his emotions through his blood relations and relatives—and he is uncertain of the reality of God.

Even though the personality may be absorbed in the ancestral stream and the materialistic interests of the world, the soul as a mediator between man and God will continue to send to the personality many reminders—through conscience and dreams—that man is more than personality. When personality fails and man falls into desperation and limitation, the instant he starts the practice of prayer he will begin his rise above the dependence upon the power of personality, and he will come to rely upon the Power of God.

A person who prays and dedicates to become a better instrument in the world comes closer to the higher expression of his individuality and to higher degrees of soul-grace.

The Father's Love is the supporting pillar for man's creation. Men move out of Him, have their being, and return to the homeplace in which He dwells and in which He ever remains. Through prayer, one may discern how men are weighed upon the scales of evil and good. He sees the mercy of God when calamities are withheld, and when men on the threshold of disasters are saved in the last hour. Spiritual instruction confirms that when men have been tried to the uttermost of their strength, then come the holy, mediative helps to aid them. Men know despair, that they may find their destiny through their souls' strength.

One who prays will come to discern that moment by moment, progress by progress, a seed of good is planted into men's minds and into their souls' light. Through prayer, the soul's light becomes more sensitive each day. One begins to recognize more and more when prayer is answered—as to its timing and as to its justice.

He who prays within the Higher Self comes to know the Father's Light and Love. When men free their hearts' loving, a true way of life will come into the earth. Love shall break asunder the walls and boundaries separating men through races, creeds, and dogmas.

Jealousy, hate, anger, superstition, and suspicion produce immoral works and sick minds. Those who pray should seek to be spiritual healers of the immoral acts in the world. When one lives within the Ethic of the Lord Jesus, he expresses love continually. His love is not as a sunrise or a sunset, or as an autumn, spring, winter, or summer: he beholds the perpetual face of love.

The soul seeks to spread its light. One who prays with dedication will hear the soul's instruction when he makes a covenant to expand the Love of God. Through the soul's instruction, he finds the Love of God within himself; the true patterns of the spiritual life begin to form within his disciplines and his works.

> *O men of the earth,*
> *Look tenderly upon life,*
> *And be thou quickened to the drama*
> *of life.*
> *There is no greater tone*
> *Than the tone of the soul's knowing.*
> *Let men be as titans,*
> *Moving aside their obstacles*
> *With spiritual law,*
> *With understanding,*
> *With vision.*

THE LORD'S PRAYER

To pray for others builds prayer power. Prayers have greater power when one does not ask to receive for himself. Selfless prayer quickens the heart atoms and keeps open the love-portals of the heart. When one prays earnestly, the angels will help him to come closer to the heart of the Lord Jesus, who taught men the words in the Lord's Prayer.

In the Lord's Prayer, Jesus gave the way to speak a selfless prayer in a proper sequence. There is no greater spiritual formula than the Lord's Prayer. Each line is powerfully compiled so as to overcome the rigidities built from many forceful and faulty acts. When the Lord's Prayer is spoken with cognizant meaningfulness, faith and works are established and become as one.

One who speaks the Lord's Prayer with reverence and deep devotion is using the prayer-formula of *praise, petition, supplication, intercession* and *praise.*

OUR FATHER WHICH ART IN HEAVEN,) HALLOWED BE THY NAME.) THY KINGDOM COME, THY WILL BE) DONE IN EARTH, AS IT IS IN HEAVEN.)	Praise
GIVE US THIS DAY OUR DAILY BREAD.)	Petition
AND FORGIVE US OUR TRESPASSES, AS) WE FORGIVE THOSE WHO TRESPASS) AGAINST US.)	Supplication
AND LEAD US NOT INTO TEMPTATION,) BUT DELIVER US FROM EVIL:)	Intercession
FOR THINE IS THE KINGDOM, AND THE) POWER, AND THE GLORY, FOR EVER.) AMEN.)	Praise

When one begins and ends his prayers with praise-words, his troubles and problems will fall away, and he will come close to the Father with a most intense love.

Praise ye the Lord. O give thanks unto the Lord;
for he is good: for his mercy endureth for ever.
—Psalms 106:1

In the petition part of prayer, one should be careful that he does not ask for something which may become a burden to himself or to others; for he should always remember that all prayers are answered.

. . . the Lord hath given me my petition which I asked of him . . .

—I Samuel 1:27

The supplication part of prayer occurs when one prays with a deep humbleness for the general good of the many. The Father will answer his supplication by making it possible for him to serve humanity in right timing and in right placement.

The Lord hath heard my supplication; the Lord will receive my prayer.

—Psalms 6:9

In the intercession part of prayer one acknowledges that the Heavenly Presences will intercede for him and protect him from temptation and evil, and that their guidance will ever be near him in times of need and peril. He will come to recognize that there are Holy Ones in Heaven who protect him. Such Holy Ones pray unceasingly for men in the world, that the feet of men stumble not, and that men be not tempted. The Angels and the Presences of Heaven work with one's prayers so that his prayers be not scattered or wasted.

. . . the Spirit itself maketh intercession for us with groanings which cannot be uttered.

—Romans 8:26

Jesus prayed on His knees. The Bible tells of prayer on the knees. When one prays on his knees, he comes closer to God with a humble heart.

O come, let us worship and bow down: let us kneel before the Lord our maker.

— Psalms 95:6

The surrender of the lesser will to the greater Will of "Our Father which art in heaven" redirects the senses and frees the soul-faculties or higher attributes of each sense. It is necessary to approach the state of prayer with a complying will, a reverent heart, and a teachable mind.

To keep rhythmic alignment in selfless prayer, one should pray on his knees three times a day. When one prays upon the knees, certain sentient atoms in the emotional body and fiery currents in the spine and heart are stilled. When one kneels in prayer and lowers his head, he enters into the womb position of surrendering himself to the origin of all life in this earth—the Father and the Will of God. The Father becomes a tangible Presence to those who, day by day, continue in the rhythmic practice of prayer on the knees.

Conscience seeks to make its voice oral through prayer. As one kneels in prayer, the heart, the conscience, and the soul are at one. When a person is not accustomed to the practice of prayer on the knees, he may at first have a feeling of physical congestion through the lungs, palpitation of the heart, and constriction of the throat. This resistance is caused by the pressures from the vibratory hum around the soul's medallion. With continued practice, prayer makes quiescent the heavy shadings of one's wrongdoing imprinted upon the vibratory hum of the soul's medallion. If one persists in prayer, the conscience will reveal what the soul wishes to speak through prayer as of the Will of God for him.

Prayer is an instrument of coordination to channel spiritual power and to make alignment with "Our Father which art in heaven." The length of prayer is determined by the belief in the efficacy of prayer, and by that which speaks spontaneously from the heart to the Father. The length of prayer is determined by a knowing within—a certain action or release, in which the one who prays knows that his prayers are being heard. Thus, one should pray until he has made a supernatural contact with the dynamic words of Jesus, who said: "Your Father knoweth what things ye have need of."

At the closing of a pure, spiritual prayer— the palms of the hands remaining together, and the eyes still closed—the head should be raised. In this, one receives the confirming response to that which has been spoken in prayer.

One should pray for at least ten people each day, increasing the number when so inclined. He should not forget the ten lepers—one remembered to be grateful for his healing.

To reap the greater benefits of prayer, one should cease looking upon others as personal antagonists. Through prayer, one learns to recognize what is speaking through unpleasant situations. He will come to receive a revealing grace within each unpleasant experience.

Faith in God as the one unfailing Source revitalizes and restores one's purpose and clarifies his vision. One should pray to transmit his faith to those with weakened foresight and intent.

CONTEMPLATION AND THE INDIVIDUALITY

When prayer has impersonalized the personality, one ceases to express his lower ancestral concepts and begins to make evident another significant phase of expression—the higher individuality. The higher individuality consists of a depth and sensitivity beyond the personality. The individuality is the compass for the talents and the dispenser of originality.

While personality is the heir to ancestral traits, the individuality is the heir to mental characteristics of former lives. A noble individuality in the present life is the heritage of innumerable pure thought patterns and creative mental activities of former lives. The individuality, when in rapport with the highest degree of thought from former lives, expresses a quality beyond genius, and answers some vital need in the world.

Pure expressive individuality is the truest reflection of the creative power of God. As the soul is the mediator for the Higher Self, the individuality is the mediator for thought. The individuality is the communicable self—a very intimate self. Contemplation is a means by which the mentality and the individuality may extend their range of communicableness. When one applies himself to contemplation, he will have access to a lucid thought action above the cunning thought; thus, the soul may illumine his thought with creative ideas. Contemplation will also enable him to penetrate the grace of his pure and creative thoughts of former lives. Through the practice of contemplation, one achieves selfless individuality devoid of egotism.

Many persons think of concentration as contemplation. One should be careful to avoid concentration—that is, the intensified use of the will in thinking upon any object, symbol, person, or circumstance.

Contemplation and meditation are often thought to be the same; however, they are different exercises. Contemplation frees the pure thought processes of former lives and of this life; meditation frees the Light activity of the soul and of the Higher Self.

When one begins the process of cleansing or eradicating all irreverent traits, he will have access to the grace earned in former lives; he will be fortified to meet the challenges and trials inevitably presented in his life. Skills, talents, and unusual aptitudes inherited from former lives' actions will also begin to reveal themselves.

The personality may be compared to a bell; the individuality, to the clapper or tongue of the bell; and the Higher Self, to the tone of the bell—for the personality, the individuality, and the Higher Self will ultimately combine to resound the Tone of God.

CONTEMPLATION

The Spirit is to the mind of man what the sun is to the earth. The soul is to the emotions what the moon is to the earth—that is, the soul reflects the Spirit as the moon reflects the sun.

The soul-will empowers one to create. The soul-life empowers one to image and to bring form to his creation. And the soul-love enables him to heal through his creation.

Contemplation is a visualizing process of illuminative thought activated by the soul. Contemplation is the essence of spiritual thinking. Pure contemplation is uncolored by sentient or personalized thinking. Pure contemplation removes the glamors of the lesser-will in thought and feeling, and aids in resolving the etheric cobwebs obstructing clarity in thought. Through contemplative thought men will eventually acquire the powers of true imaging.

In contemplation the ego's record of this life and of past lives becomes temporarily quiescent; and spiritual thoughts are free to move upon a lucid field prepared by many prayers, contemplations, and meditations in this life and in other lives.

TWO EXERCISES IN MANTRAMIC
CONTEMPLATIVE THOUGHT

I think
Of the odor of crushed violets;
Of men who walk with humility,
Brushing their shoulders with
*   humanity—*
Pure men who are known not,
But who carry the fragrances of
*   Heaven.*

I think
Of the softened petals of the rose;
And of the saint unseen
Who has given the sacred word,
And who has passed on
Without looking back—
But has given with joy.

I think
Of the autumn fragrance and
    pungency,
Of a broken twig,
Of a golden leaf,
Of the moist earth.
And I feel a nostalgia,
A longing for things unknown,
Of a seed yet to be in the earth,
Waiting to come to birth.
And I say, "O men of the earth,
Look to thy joy,
For you are goodly soil for God.
Let Him plant you;
And let him enrich you."

      *   *   *

Chaste and white is the lily.
Each petal,
In its fragrant and chaste light,
Spreads.
I look within and see
The life, love, and light.
The purity of my senses,
United with my soul,
Opens the bud of promise.

I move and blend with
    contemplation,
Assembling my thoughts—
Gathering from my heart
Reverence and holiness.

I enter into the door.
The threshold wide
Welcomes me.
Through remembrance of the old,
I walk with familiar faces
Into the dear places I have known
Through love, reverence, joy.

MEDITATION

**Let the words of my mouth, and the meditation of
my heart, be acceptable in thy sight, O Lord, my
strength, and my redeemer.**   **—Psalm 19:14**

The practice of meditation is rarely observed
by persons in formal religions, for the majority
of religions depend upon prayer as the means
to approach the Power of God. The mystic
depends upon lengthy meditation rather than
prayer to approach the Power of God. A psychical person, extending his senses material-
istically, uses concentration rather than meditation. The metaphysician uses thought-visuali-
zation rather than meditation. The occultist,
concentrating his will upon certain centers of
the body, depends upon the power of his personal will, rather than blending with the Will
of God. The esoteric person follows a formula
in dedicated meditation, preparing himself to
become a spiritual channel to the world. The
spiritual person prays, contemplates, and medi-

tates; and, thus, serves as an integral part of a great honeycomb of spiritual mediation.

Prayer, contemplative, and meditative practices are the nourishments for a spiritual life. To be shut away from spiritual food is to lose the soul's discriminating power.

Prayer orders the emotions and the physical life. Contemplation orders the thought. Meditation opens the portals of Heaven.

The soul's most sensitive attribute is the conscience. When one obeys his conscience and prays, he produces an ordered pattern in his physical life—and all situations, conditions, and things become spiritually animated and purposeful. When one contemplates, he organizes his thoughts and opens himself to receive the greater creative thoughts; thereby receiving illuminative ideas enabling him to better serve in the world. When one meditates, he extends his spiritual capacity for Light and develops a selfless love potential.

The Higher Self or Eternal Self is the Instructor of man. The Higher Self is at home in the Spiritual Worlds. To have access to or to reach the Higher Self, one should build a way or a means of communication. Until alignment is made with the Higher Self, the heart, the thought, and the soul have individual methods of communication and are often separate in their expressions. Prayer, contemplation, and meditation enable the heart, the thought, and the soul to become at one, whereby a continuity of love and light may be sustained. A telepathic rapport with the Higher Self is accomplished—and the true voice may be heard interpreting the Spiritual Worlds, the Will of God, and His Plan for man.

Through the continued practice of prayer, contemplation, and meditation, the atoms of the physical, emotional, and mental bodies are brought into alignment with the Higher Self. The great eternal laws are interpreted to the disciple, and the Higher Self becomes the logos or interpreter of the Spiritual Worlds.

Creative thought is a reality, but until a body of light has been built to sustain creative thinking, there is the danger of psychic experience. One should refrain from deeper contemplation until he has made a harmonious alignment in meditation.

Meditation is for the purpose of bringing the various atoms in all bodies into alignment, and of building and sustaining a power-body of light. During meditation there is an unseen activity which is later manifested in the outer consciousness in perfect timing to the need. This appears in a form of telepathy as guidance and instruction. In higher stages of evolvement, the archetypes may be read during the practice of meditation.

There is a difference between prayer and meditation. When one prays, he works with the Life Fiat through speech, heart, and soul. When he meditates, he works with the Light Fiat through the speaking of mantrams, the stilling of thoughts, and alignment with the Higher Self. To receive the full benefit of prayer, the practice of prayer should be in conjunction with the practice of meditation. Through the combined action of meditation and prayer, prayer will become an instrument of tremendous power with instantaneous response.

Meditation has many and varied interpretations. Some confuse meditation with contemplation; or, concentration is sometimes thought to be meditation. To apply oneself to rhythm in meditation, so as to reach an accord with the soul and with the Higher Self, requires an undeviating regularity as to timing and method. To obtain the best results in meditation, there should be a deep desire to commune with the intelligible power of the soul. Improper meditation with emphasis upon concentration sometimes causes a hazardous reaction, shocking the delicate alliance between the heart and the mind; and sometimes exposes the thought to psychical rather than spiritual experience. Tense meditation habits or practices create an enlargement of the etheric covering of the heart, unbalancing the emotional polarity and equilibrium of the feeling-world.

Meditation should be practiced in an environment of privacy and quiet. The one meditating should be seated, his eyes gently closed. To concentrate upon any one or any thing in meditation is to make the senses the perceiver; therefore, there should be no thought upon any desire or person, as this would interfere with the releasing of tension from the feeling and thinking of the one meditating. It would also interfere with the Higher Self's sending onto the magnetic field of the brain the pure telepathies and the reflections of the archetypes from the Spiritual Worlds.

Prolonged meditation is dangerous, creating an abnormal pressure upon the will. One should limit his meditation to a period of no more than five minutes. In this manner he is protected from will intensification and psychic intrusion.

A simple procedure for meditation is as follows:

1. *Place the thought and feeling, reverently and tenderly, upon the heart. Gather all the love that you feel, know, and think; and center it in the heart. Hold it firmly for a few seconds. Then replace this thought of love with light.*

2. *Raise the light to the level of the brow, and still the thought with*

light. This should not exceed a few seconds.

3. *Gently lift the light to the crown of the head, and hold the light for five minutes.*

A mantram should be spoken aloud before and after meditation. If one is unable to speak the mantram aloud, he should speak the mantram silently, forming the words with his lips.

Day unto day uttereth speech, and night unto night showeth knowledge.

Their line is gone out through all the earth, and their words to the end of the world. In them hath he set a tabernacle for the sun . . .

—Psalm 19:2,4

In meditation one becomes aware of the necessity to clear the screen of his mind and to still his thoughts. In time, critical thought will withdraw its functioning, and a holy perceiving will be attained. The one meditating will blend with the Higher Self and with the holy symbology supporting the spiritual life.

Should one feel that meditation is a labor, he should cease meditating until the desire for meditation so possesses him that he is concerned only with reaching an accord with his Higher Self and the Spiritual Worlds.

Any barrier to meditation is indicative of a preparatory period for the heavier labors in discipleship. Such barriers will continue until one's inward desire to be at one with God becomes so strong that the desire itself will set afire and burn away all karmic barriers. Then one will come into timing with the grace of his soul.

One should enter into his rhythmic meditation practices with a loving reverence, hungry for his association in Light. If he will reflect on the past days and years before he entered into these practices, he will find that he wasted many hours in fruitless tasks or in idleness.

Prayer, contemplation, and meditation order the pattern of life and budget the time, so that each moment is mediative, and therefore creative.

Meditation is the stilling of all thoughts and the holding of light. In contemplation one follows the same procedure as in meditation—*with the exception that he holds the light over the brow rather than over the crown of the head;* and after his personalized thoughts are stilled, he contemplates certain ideas, symbols, or dramas. The brow correlates directly to an eternal atom called the Indestructible Atom. This atom, which is centered in the middle of the forehead, acts as a tuning fork for contemplation. The Indestructible Atom, a tributary for the Christ Mind, sets the tone for what is received by the highly evolved disciple.

The soul is a reflector for the twelve spiritual atoms of the higher etheric body or everlasting body. The soul works in a pulsating and alternating action of expansion and contraction. The pulsation of the soul correlates to the heartbeat of the physical heart. When the heartbeat ceases at death, the pulsation of the soul becomes the heartbeat for the spiritual body within the Spiritual Worlds.

The soul of man has been perfected by Eternal Spirit. The power of the soul IS. Nothing can be added to the soul. However, one can free the soul's action by prayer, contemplation, and meditation. Prayer, contemplation, and meditation are three ways through which the soul may translate what the Higher Self would communicate or say.

> *For each tender seed,*
> *Each quickened plant,*
> *Each flowering bud,*
> *Each fruit,*
> *There is an atom of Spirit Eternal.*
> *There is a deathless immortality.*
> *For each pure thought,*
> *There is an image,*
> *An idea,*
> *An archetype.*
> *These are Eternal in God's Creation.*

For each feeling,
Each desire,
Each emotion,
There is a heart of love,
Where dwells the sacred atom of
     deathless love.
For each hope and prayer,
There is an answer.

3

GRACE

For the law was given by Moses, but grace and truth came by Jesus Christ.

—St. John 1:17

The Seven Degrees of Grace There are seven degrees of grace. These degrees of grace are supported and sustained by heavenly edicts. Innumerable facets of grace proceed from the seven degrees of grace. The soul seeks to bless and anoint each one with this magnanimity of God.

Day-by-day Grace *Day-by-day grace* or grace of the immediate action is built from selfless serving with pure intent. The immediate grace is multiplied through good works in dedicated serving, pure motive in love, true discrimination in thought. Good works and good stewardship increase one's capacity to make alignment with other degrees of grace, so that one may, in time, work in the world as a healing presence in all environments.

Creative or Transforming Grace *Creative or transforming grace* has been earned through good works and pure ethics in previous lives. This produces in one's life the virtues, and also the creative talents for art, music, writing—or creative grace may bring some special talent for serving in the world. True virtue brought from former lives determines the use of the creative talents for the good of all rather than for egotistical expression. Transforming grace enables one to adjust to change, to be flexible, to redirect neglected talents into virile avenues of original expression. Transforming grace enables one to influence others to change, or to be an instrument for changes in decaying or crystallized environments.

Sacred or Sacrifice Grace

Sacred or sacrifice grace is grace one has gathered from his former lives of martyrdom or selfless works which were devoid of thought of reward. Sacred or sacrifice grace resides within the outer portion of the Diamond Medallion around the Higher Self, and is the means through which one receives spiritual gifts. When one has made alignment with his Higher Self's action, and with the grace degree of his spiritual gifts, he manifests spiritual works and presents to the world certain knowledge and instruction gathered from his own experience in the Light.

Eternal Grace

Eternal grace is grace one has earned in other eternity systems, previous to birth in this earth. When one entered this eternity system, eternal grace was sealed into the central point of the Diamond Medallion around the Higher Self. Eternal grace is watched over by one's Recording Angel. Grace from one's actions in other eternities is spiritual power. When one makes alignment with eternal grace, he brings to the world a teaching of man's "everlasting life" as of the eternals, rather than that which pertains only to this eternity. He is able to communicate to men the imperishable knowledge of eternal or everlasting life. He belongs to that company of elect known as the *Illuminati*.

World Grace

World grace is grace earned by humanity through good works in this eternity. World grace is watched over by the greater Recording Angels known as the Angels of Judgment. This grace enables mankind to experience its Saviours. If one has alignment with world grace or the works of good of mankind, he is an adept who has commanded the gravity trials, and has made contact with the Planetary Guardian Angels of the Spheres of Light (Second Heaven). He thus works with the fulcrum energies at midnight, and also with the solstitial and equinoctial energies during the four seasons of the year.

Healing Grace

Healing grace is the grace of the love of Jesus, the Lord of Healing Grace, who dwells in the Realm of Light, the Kingdom of Heaven, or the World Medallion (Third Heaven). When one has earned the love of Jesus through spiritual proximity, he has heart-to-heart oneness with the Jesus One, the Lord of Healing Love and Grace. He stands as a mediator in the Christ Light, fulfilling the Christ Mind, and thus lives within the archetypes expressing the first degrees of creation. He has access to Melchizedek powers of transubstantiation, or the powers of de-manifestation and manifestation.

Divine Grace

Divine grace is God's Will for man. If one comes under divine grace, he seals into himself certain hierarchy powers, in which the Cosmos realities or World of the Eternals are opened to him. Divine grace enables one to have access to the Divine Beings overdwelling this eternity. When one has divine grace, his person becomes a presence for God. He has prescient and omniscient powers. To be healed under divine grace is to be healed for all time. When one comes under divine grace, he enters into a life of utter sanctification and good. One who possesses divine grace is destined to fulfill the Will of God. His actions belong not to himself—as he is purposed to be a catalyst for God. His acts are the blueprints for men to follow in aeons yet unborn.

> *My soul is a lantern lit of God.*
> *My soul is a seeker, seeking to*
> *make earth Heaven.*
> *My soul is a voice waiting to speak*
> *of eternal things.*
> *My soul is a household awaiting*
> *its master.*
> *My soul is a threshold inviting*
> *the stranger.*

*My soul is a wanderer homesick
for the eternals.
My soul is a door awaiting
the key.*

I will praise thee; for I am fearfully and wonderfully made: marvelous are thy works; and that my soul knoweth right well.
— Psalm 139:14

The Golden Veil of the Soul

The golden veil of the soul, the golden habitation of the soul, the golden vision of the soul, the golden tangibles of the soul, the golden immunity of the soul, and the golden temple of the soul—these are a reality to him who would seek to know the soul.

Men are futile in their despairings, sordid in their little wills, and timorous when they know not the truth—and they are awkward vessels when they use truth wrongly.

The golden veil of the soul is protection against men who would slay or persecute, and gives the last-hour helps when all seems lost. The golden habitation of the soul is the home-place of the soul in Heaven. All men yearn for the quiet and the peace of the habitation of the soul. Men enter into the golden habitation of the soul through meditation.

The golden vision of the soul has been given to all men of the earth, upon their entry into the earth. The golden tangibles of the soul are the earnings of pure grace in other lives. The golden immunity of the soul is attained when one has stood in the hallowed Light of saintly works. The golden temple of the soul is a soul-mansion of pure and perfect Light, reflecting

the sacred sacraments where the worship and
adoration of God are sustained.

> *I give thanks for the built-in*
> *   protections*
> *provided by the veil of my soul.*
> *May my foolishness harm no one.*
> *May my right-doing set aright*
> *the folly of my unknowing.*
>
> *

> *I acknowledge the illimitable,*
> *eternal power of my soul.*
> *And I recognize my own will*
> *to be yet a novice*
> *in this eternity system.*

I counsel thee to buy of me gold tried in the fire, that thou mayest be rich; and white raiment, that thou mayest be clothed, and that the shame of thy nakedness do not appear; and anoint thine eyes with eyesalve, that thou mayest see.

—Revelation 3:18

Garment of the Soul's Grace

The soul ceases not in its search for the perfect garment to wear. He who would wear a garment unworthy of the soul substitutes the false for the real, and thus invites disparagement. His sufferings and despairs are caused by his failure to discern the difference between the unreal and the real.

He who would wear the garment of the soul's valor and grace must earn his grace moment by moment and hour by hour. He who would wear the higher garment of light must each day increase his capacity to think with light, work with light, to see all things in the light.

When grace is earned, the soul stands in its perfect garment; spiritual harmony begins, and peace is unconfined. Gather the golden jewels of thy grace and put on thy garment of peace. And thou shalt have the increase, the extending and expanding grace.

The heat of my passions
and the excitations of my senses
obscure my grace.

*May I temper my will
in the fiery purification
of perfect reliance on God.*

*

*I pray to face my sorrows and
disappointments
with equanimity,
for I would come face to face
with my comfort grace.*

*

*My militant will
is a stormy cloud
veiling away the Will of God.
May I be gentle,
yielding, kind.*

*

*My safe-going comes
from protective grace.
I give thanks for the blessed
protective helps.*

*

*My grace is more than luck,
more than good fortune.
My grace is my providence,
providing the way,
the plan.*

But he giveth more grace. Wherefore he saith,
God resisteth the proud, but giveth grace unto the
humble.
                                        —James 4:6

Soul-
Grace
and
Reverence

The grace of the soul is acquired through selfless and good works over many lives. To work with the highest degree of soul-grace requires a reverent heart and a non-critical and spiritually discriminating mind. A continuing state of reverence will sustain the grace of the soul, and thus will enable the disciple to become the recipient of creative and inspiring talents—opening the way to overcome restrictions in environment and in personal association.

The disciple should revere the sacred rights of persons as to their personality, individuality, and spirituality. And he should respect their possessions, expressions, and right of choice as to their faith and worship. Through such actions and attitudes, he will make true mediative alignment with his own soul-grace and with the soul-grace of others.

A person may stifle and veil his soul-grace by imaging or desiring objects little needed in his evolvement. The soul-grace is abused when one seeks to use the powers and gifts of the soul to sustain the wrongdoing of another. And the gifts of the soul-grace may be depleted through indulgence, inertia, procrastination. When a person recklessly squanders his soul-grace, he thwarts his creative talents and devitalizes his inspiration. Such a person will find himself dependent solely on his intellectuality and his personality for expression.

Soul-grace works with alternating rhythms. To balance and sustain the action of soul-grace, there should be, each day, some effort made to selflessly apply the works of grace for the good in the world. In this manner, the soul-grace is renewed in perfect timing.

How wondrous is the weaving of
    the threads
in my soul-garment.
And how beautiful is the design of
    my creation.

I will sing of the mercies of the Lord forever: with my mouth will I make known thy fruitfulness to all generations.
—Psalm 89:1

Benign Grace and the Magnet of Light

A reverent and humble person may be surprised or even astonished when he becomes the receiver of some gesture of selfless good. Such good is the bread of a former day returned upon the waters of grace. All kind acts and tender considerations are *magnets of light* and inevitably return in time of crisis or need. Many persons, although destitute, retain a glimmer of hope in the immortal essence of good, for within their hearts is an innate faith in the Plan of God.

The disciple is the receiver of Benign Grace when he has more than mercy for his fellow men, more than charity for the weak. Benign Grace will enable him to call upon the wisdom of right discrimination and true perception, so that his prayers and efforts go not astray. Benign Grace enables him to see beyond the outer circumstance. He will look, with his heart, into the heart of things.

The Benign Grace of the soul releases the oil of preciousness upon the wounds and scars of folly. The ministering to the unthinking requires patience plus insight. Those who follow the darkened magnet fall in the world; and those who follow the magnet of light must work to lift them. The Benign Angels assist the serving disciples, that the disciples may waver not in their ministering.

> *My sympathies*
> *seek to be more compassionate*
> *each day.*
> *Today I shall fill my heart*
> *with tenderness and understanding,*
> *for I would heal*
> *the wounds of separateness.*

For whosoever hath, to him shall be given, and he
shall have more abundance: but whosoever hath
not, from him shall be taken away even that he
hath.
—St. Matthew 13:12

**Soul-
Grace**
Soul-grace may come to one in many beneficial ways. However, if one abuses his soul-
grace, it is removed from him; and though he
cry out and yearn, there is no one to hear except
an empty echo of his need.

One squanders his soul-grace when he abuses
his body through bad habits, and also by offences
against the purity of the physical body. One
squanders his grace of money when he abuses
his stewardship by using money to rule another.
When one fails to be grateful for at least one
true friend, or even two or three spiritual
friends met in His name, he squanders the soul-
grace presented to him in perfect relationship.
When this is done, he must earn "seventy times
seven" before he can again receive the soul-grace
of perfect friendship.

One also may squander his soul-grace when
he touches the spiritual life and receives the
benefit of spiritual teachings and fails to apply
the words given to him spiritually.

One can depend upon God's equation at all
times. God's equation works with exactness,
justice. When one lacks any thing, he should
seek to research and analyze his stewardship.

And he should determine to hold—with delicacy, faith, integrity and ethic—that which is given to him through soul-grace.

I will try to preserve
and use wisely my grace,
for I remember that God's equation
knows not partiality.
"For He . . . sendeth the rain on
the just
and on the unjust."

*

There are five bountifuls:
the good, the merciful, the true,
the pure, the beautiful.
May I receive them.

*

My balm of Gilead is a precious
balm
residing within my heart, my soul.
My grace is a healer,
a peacemaker, a joy-giver.

*

How may the healing come
when waste has laid low
my plan of good?
Let me be not a victim
of wanton waste.

And the foundations of the wall of the city were garnished with 'all manner of precious stones. The first foundation was jasper; the second, sapphire; the third, a chalcedony; the fourth, an emerald; the fifth, sardonyx; the sixth, sardius; the seventh, chrysolyte; the eighth, beryl; the ninth, a topaz; the tenth, a chrysoprasus; the eleventh, a jacinth; the twelfth, an amethyst.

—Revelation 21:19,20

The Unseen Jewel of the Soul

He who wears the unseen jewel of the soul may pass over the threshold of Heaven into the upper chambers of instruction. Each life contains this mysterious and unseen jewel of the soul—a jewel created not by the hand of man, but by a sacred alchemy between the soul and the Spirit.

When one becomes aware of his unseen jewel, he enters into a radiant glory in heart and in mind. In the physical world, the jewel shines forth through the garment of stability, integrity, honor, ethic. The unseen jewel of the soul brings joy to him who has earned it, peace to him who beholds it, and a perpetual blessing to him who wears it.

May my heart and my mind
become a flawless frame
for the setting of my unseen jewel.

*

I behold the Equation of God
when I come nigh unto my soul.

*

When I meditate,
each atom within my spiritual
    body
becomes a facet
of my unseen jewel.

*

May the warming flame in my
    heart
ignite and burn away
the barriers obscuring
the unseen jewel of my soul.

Behold, I give unto you power to tread on serpents
and scorpions, and over all the power of the enemy:
and nothing shall by any means hurt you. Notwith-
standing in this rejoice not, that the spirits are
subject unto you; but rather rejoice, because your
names are written in heaven.

—St. Luke 10:19,20

The
Treasures
of Grace   All pure and good works are the products of
a proven heart and mind. The disciple is the
steward of the treasures or grace of his soul.
However, he may endanger the treasures or
grace of his soul by failing to acknowledge his
beliefs, failing to live his beliefs, or permitting
someone to repress his beliefs.

The immortal record of the soul is renewed
from life to life. No outer condition or person
can erase the record of grace from the soul's
medallion unless consent is given. The sacrifices
asked of the disciple day by day, and even the
little desires yielded up for the sake of others,
sustain the grace of the soul and make the disciple eligible to receive his record of grace. To
consent to the repression of one's spiritual life
will deter and prevent one from receiving the
higher degrees of his grace.

When the disciple, through repeated prayers
and contemplations, has made alignment with
his soul, and is convinced of the reality of the
spiritual life, the challenger comes forth to
search him. Very often, this occurs through

some closely associated person. Let the disciple be alert and forget not these words of Jesus:

> **And fear not them which kill the body, but are not able to kill the soul: but rather fear him which is able to destroy both soul and body in hell.**
>
> **—St. Matthew 10:28**

If the disciple reaffirms his faith in the power of God within the soul, his words are heard on all Mediation levels. Instantaneously, he will become aware of the mighty channelings of strength fortifying his action. Thus the challenger is overcome.

My song on this day
is one of victory,
for I have awakened
to the meaning
of the Living Spirit.

          *

The ruby red of my heart's flame
stirs again.
And I shall be renewed
through the soul's
immortal good.

But why dost thou judge thy brother? or why dost thou set at nought thy brother? for we shall all stand before the judgment seat of Christ. For it is written, As I live, saith the Lord, every knee shall bow to me, and every tongue shall confess to God.

—Romans 14:10,11

Soul-Grace and Timing

When harmony and timing are one, there is a soul resonance—and the grace of the soul is free to work the works of God, to create and to manifest.

Soul-grace is especially dependent upon the action of the will. To express the lesser will through force, or to seek to obtain things for the self through overzealousness is to create dissonance or discord. Hasty action defeats the rhythmic timing of the soul's action, and will result in an imbalance of the rhythmic and cyclic element in timing. All accidents, worldly sorrows, and the majority of sicknesses are the result of inverse or abused timing.

The disciple should seek to free the soul's grace through simplification and order in all things presented to him. He should dwell often upon the thought of his ethic seeking to reveal itself to him. He should rely wholly upon the great formulas of Jesus, and he should seek to fulfill the greater laws of God. Timing—when used rhythmically as to order, ethic, formula, law, archetype—will produce perfect perception, discrimination, and coordination as to Nature, man, and the Will of God.

Procrastination is a deadly foe of the disciple. The disciple begins to express his fullest spiritual capacity when he removes the obstacle of procrastination. The Guardian Angel will work with the disciple's initiatory process to help him to overcome the hindering influences of the crystallized and rigid habits of many lives, which have built into him a certain unresponsiveness to his soul-grace. The disciple should call upon his Guardian Angel to help him so that, step by step, he may overcome this veil of restraint defeating the rhythmic order and timing for the receiving of soul-grace.

I shall not vacillate,
nor shall I make hasty decision.
I shall place my will
into the light of Wisdom's revealing.

*

My soul, radiant in its lightest
    Light,
times my works, my will.
And I am free from confused
    convictions
which would retard each moment
    and hour of preciousness.

My soul melteth for heaviness: strengthen thou
me according unto thy word.

— Psalm 119:28

Crisis and
the Soul
The greater spiritual, rhythmic law within crises is seldom understood. Each physical, emotional, and mental crisis is a pause in time, so that the person involved may enter into a higher relating with the powers of his soul. In each greater crisis there is to be found a precious pearl of wisdom, a renewed strength and stamina.

Some persons experience one crisis after another, because in former lives they have been lethargic. Other persons, who live in their self-engrossment and satisfactions, often find themselves catapulted into situations for which they are unprepared. Only radical crises may resolve crystallization. Greater crises, or long and sustained periods of desperation, open the portals to hidden talents or genius, thereby removing the former burdens causing anxiety.

The soul Is, even as God Is. The soul cannot be developed, shaped, or changed. However, the powers of the soul enable each person to change, grow, develop, and evolve. From transitory action and change, a person grows or develops. Change, growth, and development are the results of the cyclic law or gravity law working indirectly with the powers of the soul. *Evolvement* is the result of a more direct alignment with the powers of the soul.

From crises correlated to the rhythmic law, a person evolves. Evolvement is produced by major and significant occurrences in the life of a person spiritually inclined. These occurrences or crisis periods are climactic, catalyst, or crucial trials in the life of the spiritual disciple. From such crisis periods the disciple obtains a closer communion with the World of God and extends his capacity to observe the undeviating laws of God.

*Today's creation is tomorrow's
    preparation.
My soul shall harmonize
the Beatitudes and the promise of
    the new day;
and I will be born again.*

*

*My yesterday's seed, planted
    with love,
works for me within the reservoir
    of my soul.
I shall reap my bountiful harvest
    of grace with graciousness.*

For I long to see you, that I may impart unto you
some spiritual gift, to the end ye may be established . . .
                                          —Romans 1:11

We then, as workers together with him, beseech
you also that ye receive not the grace of God in
vain. (For he saith, I have heard thee in a time
accepted, and in the day of salvation have I suc-
coured thee: behold, now is the accepted time;
behold, now is the day of salvation.)
                                      —II Corinthians 6:1,2

Gifts of the Soul The soul is an aeon-harp upon which God
sounds His Tone, His Word. When the "ac-
cepted time" is near, the teacher appears who
holds the key to the disciple's talents, his grace,
and the gifts of his soul.

All talents have been earned through ethical
skills in former lives. Grace has been earned
through sacrificial acts. Gifts of the soul are
acquired through universal and eternal grace.

When a true teacher or teaching quickens the
gifts of the soul, the Word of God takes possession of one's faculties; henceforth his purpose
is to heed the Word of God and to serve Him.

My soul gifts
are holy mediators for God.

*

My hand has loosed the thread
binding my treasure.
I shout for joy,

for I am now a soul-gift steward
for God.

*

May I practice the first rules:
self-control and self-reliance.
For I would express the third
    rule—charity;
and thus become free
to express my soul gifts.

*

My angel has been patient
with my dallying.
My soul waits to give me more
    of Light.
May my tempo be quickened,
so that I may know and act
as an ethical one for God.

The heavens declare the glory of God; and the firmament sheweth his handywork.
—Psalm 19:1

Protection
Grace

The soul seeks to write the history of Heaven upon the mind. The soul speaks of Heaven and its territories, its various parts and communities. When one understands what the soul has to say concerning Heaven, he becomes a holy personage in earth.

If one has received Protection Grace in former lives, he is aware of Heaven, and he enlarges the vision of Heaven for other men. One should be patient with those who know not Heaven or who believe not on Heaven.

Knowledge of Heaven must be earned. After having earned the knowledge of Heaven, one uses his grace to be a peacemaker, a joy-bringer. One who speaks of Heaven is considered a cornerstone, a pillar for God. Only the love-tongue can speak of Heaven and be heard. The soul would teach one to be more loving, that he might speak freely of the reality of Heaven.

*O my soul, thou art my computer
and my perfect assessor.*

*

*Blessed is he
who has been transfixed by
Heaven's Light.*

*

*May I earn the grace of
    graciousness,
for I would wound not.*

*

*I shall listen to the tender
    reminders,
the gentle nudges from my soul.
I shall hear my soul's counsel,
and obey.*

He that overcometh shall inherit all things; and
I will be his God, and he shall be my son.
—Revelations 21:7

**Posterity
Grace**

The greater truths are preserved from age to
age through Posterity Grace. Through Posterity
Grace, men are led and guided toward the
thresholds of immortality.

To be a bestower of Posterity Grace, one must
have had countless days and months of communion with the reality of the Higher Worlds.
Thus, his thoughts, as seeds, are implanted into
the receiving fertility of those who eagerly prepare themselves for works within the Light.

Posterity Grace is the grace a pure teacher
bequeaths to his disciples. To increase Posterity
Grace, one blends the spiritual experience of
this life with the veneration and wisdom
achieved throughout many lives of sacred dedication and devotion to God.

*My works of good
have an adhering immortality.
I call on my good,
and aspire to the works of good
for the good of all.*

*

*May my devotion become
the sacred cloak of love-giving.
And may my spiritual shadow, or
Light of the Higher Self,*

fall upon those who know not,
and stir them to peace, hope, faith.

*

How bitter is the portion of him
who is faithless to good.
Let my words of good be unpolluted
by what my ears report
of men's non-Niscience or
non-knowing.

*

To channel my good,
I shall seek to forgive "seventy
times seven."
And I shall see immediately,
quickly,
the result of my trying.

But grow in grace, and in the knowledge of our
Lord and Saviour Jesus Christ. To him be glory
both now and for ever. Amen.

—II Peter 3:18

Felicity
Grace

When one seeks to rise above the darkened
way, he yields up the hidden debris pressing
against the soul's effulgent light. For every
error, there is rectification. For each stigma,
there is an anointing balm. Felicity Grace enters
into the heart; and the heart ceases its quiver—
its ache of fear and dread. Felicity Grace is the
mercy of the Father united with the compassion
of Jesus and with the understanding sent forth
from the innumerable Holy Presences of
Heaven.

Felicity Grace heals one who, by unknowing
excess, has wastefully spent his acts, works, and
ways. When one becomes totally weary of the
erroneous way, Felicity Grace tenderly covers
the imprudent heart; cleansing enters in;
strength returns. For God wastes not. In the
Equation of God, all men are born to be purposeful, fruitful. Felicity Grace is manifested
in the outer world as forgiveness toward one
another.

My soul is the perfect
mathematician—
defining, refining.
I will accept the day-by-day
results of my actions,

for I would become authored
by God's Veracity.

*

How foolish can one be
to confuse sensuousness with joy?
Peace; be still, little sentience—
for I seek a perfect love
at rest within the Love
of God.

*

I work for joy.
As the song of the lark followeth
        its flight,
so shall my joy arise and sing.

The watchmen that go about the city found me: to whom I said, Saw ye him whom my soul loveth? It was but a little that I passed from them, but I found him whom my soul loveth: I held him, and would not let him go, until I had brought him into my mother's house, and into the chamber of her that conceived me.

—Song of Solomon 3:3,4

Chastity Grace

The Life Spirit is animate in all living things. In the mountains, the Life Spirit is mineral fire. In the plants, the Life Spirit is etheric fire. In the animal, the Life Spirit is sentient fire. In man, the Life Spirit is the fire of consciousness. When one consecrates himself to the Life Spirit, and sacredly portrays the Life Spirit through spiritual works and actions, he receives the grace of chastity residing in the medallion of the Higher Self; and he is free from the sub-sentient drives seeking to enter into the feelings and thoughts. When one nobly consecrates his physical works and actions, he has the power to free the grace of his many virtues residing in the record of his soul's medallion.

Sacrificial works and deliberate actions of good etch the grace of virtue upon the soul's medallion. Purity in emotional motive, and sincerity in mental intent free the Chastity Grace dwelling around the Higher Self. The grace within the medallion of the soul records the virtue of former lives and of this life. The grace residing around the medallion of the

Higher Self reflects the innate chastity of a
person, and records the chaste, pure and passion-
less intent of all acts of consecration.

> *I prepare each day for the*
> *   Bridegroom (Christ),*
> *and for the wedding of my body*
> *   and works,*
> *my heart and mind, my soul and*
> *   spirit.*

*

> *The many paths of initiation are*
> *   revealed to me.*
> *I am at one with the many who*
> *   earn and learn—*
> *and yearn for God.*

*

> *I shall remove the yoke of*
> *   heaviness*
> *and assume the urn of the*
> *   cleansing peace.*
> *How bright are my days;*
> *for darkness has ceased*
> *now that Light has come.*

But this I say, He which soweth sparingly shall reap
also sparingly; and he which soweth bountifully
shall reap also bountifully. Every man as he pur-
poseth in his heart, so let him give; not grudgingly,
or of necessity: for God loveth a cheerful giver.
And God is able to make all grace abound toward
you; that ye, always having all sufficiency in all
things, may abound to every good work: As it is
written, He hath dispersed abroad; he hath given
to the poor: his righteousness remaineth for ever.

—II Corinthians 9:6-9

**I.
Provident
Grace**

One should seek to become acquainted with
his angels, so that they might teach him of the
treasures of his soul—for the angels have
guardianship over the treasures of the soul.
When one begins to know his angels as familiar
companions, the angels will pull aside the veil
of the treasures of the soul; and he shall doubt
not himself. And he shall stand before any man
with the treasures of his soul gathered out of
the days in which he has worked for God. No
longer shall he doubt the reality of the love
and provident intent of God for him.

He who has earned Provident Grace shall
spend his Cornucopia of Substance with magnanimity. His Cornucopia shall move with
clockwise action, timed to the need; and he will
henceforth receive the bounteous substance in
season, rhythmically, perfectly.

When a person gives to obtain, the Cornucopia of Substance works in a contraclockwise

manner. Such persons give through the smaller
end of the Cornucopia—and the Cornucopia of
Substance yields a miserly and frugal giving.
Having neither good stewardship nor the vision
to behold the magnanimity of the Substance of
God, they are impoverished and improvident.

Giving without thought of return to the giver
will in time reverse the contraclockwise action
of the Cornucopia—and one will be blessed by
the Cornucopia of Substance as given of God.

For each fruit (good) I harvest,
I shall plant a new seed.
I shall share my good.
For I know I return to God, the
Giver, when I give.

*

May my Provident Grace send me
to the place
where my talents may make more
noble
my stewardship for God.

*

If there are those who are
dependent upon me,
I give thanks that my grace
knoweth
that I am nigh to the treasures of
my soul.

*

Let me remember
that the most profound
and mighty Provident Grace
is the gift of life—
given of God.

> Beloved, I wish above all things that thou mayest prosper and be in health, even as thy soul prospereth.
>
> —3 John 1:2

**II.
Provident
Grace**

He who would obtain mastery of himself is masterful. He who would press, and use pressure, is forceful. Force is that negative which burns. Force cannot work with the Light; but force works with the electric. Where there is force and the electric, this is of the dark. When one stands in the Christ Light, he is at peace with all things as they are.

When there is unruly desire, then come many abnormalities. When the soul is free to express true desire, the desire will correctly relate itself to the need. Then shall the laws governing substance bless one, and providence shall be by his side. From this comes the Cornucopia Grace—that is, the Provident Grace. Provident Grace has been earned in former times in which one did not waste the substance of God.

*From acts of providence, wisdom,
    generosity,
I have earned my Provident Grace.*

*

*As a tender child gives,
so may I give.*

*

*May I offend not the ethic
of giving and receiving.*

*

*May I become a faithful steward,
a giver of self.
Let all my doing
be giving.*

And Enoch also, the seventh from Adam, prophesied
of these, saying, Behold the Lord cometh with ten
thousands of his Saints.
—Jude 1:14

**Sanctifi-
cation
Grace**

All tender, pure things are an extension of
God's eternal good. All true things are the right
arm of God's purposeful plan for man. The
sacred musics of Heaven unite with the saintly
rejoicings which resound for the victorious
ones who stand for the good, for the true. One
of the most beautiful musics in Heaven is the
resounding praises of the most dear Saints.

Saints are made through day-by-day grace.
From the dankest, most darkened trials, Saints
have risen to victory.

The shining light of a sacred action produces
Sanctification Grace. Each work of overcoming through faith in good, each gesture of giving through selfless sacrifice, produces Sanctification Grace. Through Sanctification Grace
the disciple is anointed. Sanctification Grace
enables one to abhor impure ways, to adore the
good. To be able to define what is good, what
is pure, is Sanctification Grace.

To do all things with harmony, to be inoffensive, to be nonintrusive upon another's
good—this solicits the helps of the greater
Saints, whose love, prayers, and sponsorships
are forever seeking to find one upon whom they
may send their Sanctification Grace.

The Saints hear the solicitations of those who have risen above the calumnies of corruption. The inoffensive, having submitted their wills to the Will of God, receive the strengths of the greater Saints.

To come under the mantle of the greater Saints, and to receive Sanctification Grace or helps from the Saints, one should be chaste, selfless, forceless, tender, good, and consistently open to Heaven.

Each Saint emanates a very special degree of grace. When one approaches the path of worthiness, he comes under the supervision of the Saint who is en rapport with his love, with his need.

Through Sanctification Grace one is sponsored by a Saint or a community of Saints; he thus enters the trials of Sainthood. Sanctification Grace enables him to bear his trials under all circumstances.

When good is victorious, the Saints shower their love upon the good. When merciful works are manifested, the Saints proclaim God's mercy to man—and the sanctification unctions of healing pour forth upon the lifted heads of those who pray for the good of the world.

O goodly ones,
O company so close to the angels,
let me rest my trust
upon the wings
of thy encouragement.

Bear with me,
for I would be closer
to thy hum and thrum
of everlasting good.

4

CONSCIENCE AND THE SOUL

Hear counsel, and receive instruction that thou
mayest be wise in thy latter end.
—Proverbs 19:20

The
Counsel
of the
Soul

All great sages and teachers are at one with the counsel of their souls. When one stands in the presence of a pure teacher, he is often aware of the nonnecessity of certain careless statements or words. Also, when one speaks of desire in the presence of such great personages, the desire echoes back to him as trivial, absurd, and of small consequence. One who comes to rely upon the counsel of his soul speaks each word with vision and meaning; and he acts upon each thing with wisdom. Thus, he avoids the pitfalls which come to those who refuse to hear the counsel of their souls.

Were it not for the soul's continually seeking to remind man that he is more than physical, all in the earth would have long since degenerated into oblivion. The soul's repeated reminders and lessons are placed before the disciple that he may come to perceive the inner meaning within his evolvement, and thereby become at one with the counsel of his soul. The soul is then free to remind him that he is more than physical.

To be satisfied with the appearance of things, rather than to seek to know or learn *what* they are and *why* they are, produces a blind, inert, and retrogressive action. There is no greater enslavement than to be encumbered with the belief that the appearance of things is the only reality in life. Only pain and unhappiness can result from dependence upon the surface issues of life. When a person is animated, inspired, and afire with a pure love for all life, life will be disclosed to him in its inner proportion and perspective. All who work to serve in the world must obtain vision, so that they may see and serve the true, rather than the surface desires of men. True vision is acquired by the searching heart. When the heart, rather than the intellect, is the searcher, the soul will distribute the light and vision into the heart and mind.

> *The immortal stair is built from*
> *   the ascent*
> *of those who have walked*
> *the perfect path of enlightenment.*
> *I fear not the climb,*
> *for I know my angel doth light*
> *   the way*
> *until my own Inner Light*
> *shall make firm my faltering steps.*

I will greatly praise the Lord with my mouth; yea,
I will praise him among the multitude.

—Psalm 109:30

Grace Tones of the Soul

The grace tones of the soul direct the harmony in the spiritual life. When the heart responds to the grace tones of the soul, love is expanded. When the mind responds to the grace tones of the soul, one thinks holy and sacred thoughts. When one is bitter, he shuts away the grace tones resounding from Heaven.

When the body responds to the sound within the grace tones, it becomes a temple of health, a true vessel for the Spirit. One should learn to enter into doors of harmony, and hear what the grace tones are saying to the body, to the mind. From this will come quietness—an inner quiet, or the supreme silence.

When the quiet in the soul's tone blends with and responds to the tone of the true, the tongue will become "the pen of a ready writer" for God.

Pure logos or speech is a gift of grace. Mantramic sayings, pure sayings, true sayings, worthy vows, dedications, covenants, and contemplations are the beginning of pure and true logos.

My peace words
are the come-home portions
of the true.

*

*How wondrous the grace
to see and to hear words of love.*

*

*Love is the levitation power
over the wounds of gravity.*

*

*I pray to come under the grace
   anointing.
To be free of vain speech
is victory.*

The law of the Lord is perfect, converting the soul: the testimony of the Lord is sure, making wise the simple.
                                    —Psalm 19:7

The Testimony of the Soul

The testimony of the soul *is* perfect. One can depend upon the testimony of the soul to tell him of the gentle way. When one adheres to the testimony of the soul, he is gentle but also firm. The gentle-firm way of the soul's testimony produces an absolute faith, which is the greatest strength in the world—greater than any physical or violent force.

The moral strength in a person comes from absolute faith in God. When the diadem of one's soul-light has been quickened, this becomes a sanctuary finer than any cathedral in the world.

There is nothing greater than the splendor of God in the soul of man. The testimony of the soul speaks continuously of this splendor. When one permits the splendor of God to shine forth in his life, the pattern of his life becomes a simple pattern—a pattern of purity, love, mercy, tenderness, peace.

May my words and works
be a testimonial flame
to the Father within me.

*

This I know and testify to:
God Is.
                        *

Healing shall come,
for the calming splendor of my
   soul
shall obscure the darkness.

Jesus saith unto them, My meat is to do the will
of him that sent me, and to finish his work. Say
not ye, There are yet four months, and then cometh
the harvest? behold I say unto you, Lift up your
eyes, and look on the fields; for they are white
already to harvest.
—St. John 4:34,35

**Spiritual
Vision**
A million mirages, thousands of chimeras,
and countless illusions must be shattered before
one may attain the spiritual vision. Spiritual
blindness is spiritual poverty. When one continues to deny God as the Theme-Mover and
Maker of the universe, his vision is shadowed,
opaque.

When the vision is upon self alone and self
concerns, one lives in a mirage of separateness.
When vision is distorted by fallible perception,
one becomes the victim of egotistical chimeras.
When one trusts only in what he can see, his
days are filled with unreality.

If there be equanimity between the heart, the
mind, the soul, and the spirit, illumination is
activated within the soul; and one sees the
World of God and the world of man with
clarity. When one sees or beholds God in the
minute and the mighty, his lips will articulate
what he sees, and he will speak benevolent and
inspiring words to those who would hear.

*My first breath at birth
gave me physical life.*

*My first vision of God and His
    works
gave me Heaven.*

*

*May my vision
be anointed by the Angels of Light,
whose name is Celestial.*

*

*The angel tells me
God hath placed His sight
upon my going in and coming out.
Therefore, my time is set to the
    Eternal Way
and my walk is of the Light.*

Come and hear, all ye that fear God, and I will declare what he hath done for my soul.

—Psalm 66:16

Speech
of the
Soul

Every man has his destiny in the world, but every man has a way in which he must fulfill this destiny through that which speaks within his soul. When many pure souls work in unison for a single purpose, this is spiritual power.

The soul is the great searchlight of the mind. When one uses the speech of the soul, he becomes as an axis in the earth. This sometimes results in a violent tremor or resistance in his outer world. When one speaks words of love with conviction, his soul opens the door to Eternal Light.

*May my speech and my timing
become one,
for I would heal the breach
of words said beyond recall.*

*

*If I cannot add
to the joy of the world,
let me be silent
until my soul sings again.*

*

*May I learn the difference
between conversation
and true speaking.*

*

When I have mastered
the mantramic words,
the tone of the archetype
shall make my mouth
a sweet well of Heaven.

Wherefore lay apart all filthiness and superfluity of naughtiness, and receive with meekness the engrafted word, which is able to save your souls.

—James 1:21

Pure
Mantrams
and the
Soul

The vibratory hum of the soul is stilled, and the grace of the soul is activated, when a mantram is spoken in right timing, right emotional releasing, and right relinquishing.

A pure mantram is the highest form of the enunciated word. When a mantram is correctly spoken, there are breathing spaces between the paramount words; spiritually potent, minute rest interludes enable the higher degrees of Light to manifest through the spoken word. When a mantram is perfectly spoken, the healing grace within the soul bursts forth in a glory of the first magnitude.

Following pure mantramic speaking, one is born anew—and there will come a divine perception, a healing, a correction.

When I create in the present,
I balance my past.

*

My thoughts are diamond points
of transubstantiation.

*

Over the aeons I have mastered
living energies of the world.
I now work to master
the eternal verities of the Spirit.

My soul shall make her boast in the Lord; the
humble shall hear thereof, and be glad.

—Psalm 34:2

Let my soul live, and it shall praise thee; and let
thy judgments help me.

—Psalm 119:175

**Praise
and the
Soul**

The soul is a praise-harp for God. By continually praising God, by constantly giving
praise for life, the Presence of God will manifest within the soul. The Ministering Angels
come nigh to the praise-giver. One who prays
for closer proximity to the Presence of God
comes under the wise counsel of the mediative
helps of Heaven.

The soul is an instrument for joy. For every
sorrow, there is a mediative comfort. For every
self-denial, there is a gift from the soul. The
Presence of God would enter into the soul, the
heart, and the mind. The doorway to the
Presence of God is the soul.

*How may I deny Thee,
for Thou art everywhere.*

*

*My soul is one of Thy universes,
and my ways cannot stray from
Thee.*

How long shall I take counsel in my soul, having sorrow in my heart daily? how long shall mine enemy be exalted over me?
        —Psalm 13:2

Holy Ingenuity

He who expresses passivity creates a tension and a recoil. But he who has the grace of blending knows the mood in each thing. When one enters into tantrums, he takes unto himself bitter portions. The flowering promise of peace is as a fragrant flower, healing the moods of bitterness, irritation, anger.

The soul provides each one with a pace-maker. When one fails to observe his soul's timing, he is held accountable for his neglect. He finds himself in unbearable situations which inflict anguish upon his thoughts and emotions. To acquire the stricter precepts of the soul, one is cleansed of passivity. This enables him to use the higher will through noble incentive, and to learn to image through the soul's intuition. Blessed is the one who undergoes the divine acceleration of the soul, for he develops a holy ingenuity, and becomes an instrument of Light.

The essence emanating from good
     works
is as a sweet savor,
comforting my heart,
my mind.

                    *

I am grateful
that my angel did teach me
the good patience,

for at last
I am learning to plant my seeds
in right season.

Our soul waiteth for the Lord: he is our help and
our shield. For our heart shall rejoice in him, because we have trusted in his holy name. Let thy
mercy, O Lord, be upon us according as we hope
in thee.   —Psalm 33:20-22

The
Miracu-
lous and
the Soul

He who seeks to manifest before timing, works
with magic. He who seeks to manifest in timing
works with the Law of God, and produces the
miraculous. When one presses to gain or obtain
out of timing, the powers of magic are activated;
he unconsciously invokes the sub-elemental and
magical forces. Thus, he receives in part; and
the heavy lessons involved must be repeated
again and again.

When one works within the rhythmic timing
of his soul, and proportions his creation within
the Equation of God, he works within the Good
Law. The results are miraculous, as each degree
of his creation is in perfect accord with the
physical, emotional, mental, and spiritual levels
of expression. The results are expressed peace-
ably in the physical, joyously in the emotional,
illuminatively in the mental, and divinely within
the spiritual.

One should learn to bend with the blows, and
to blend with the ebb and flow of the soul. In
this he will be related to timing, to faithfulness,
to obedience. He will live the good life in
Christ—and the Good Law shall teach him of
the miraculous.

My soul resideth nigh an Angel
     of Hope.
I shall be hospitable
toward my good Angel.

*

May the heavy tares be removed
in right timing.
I will bear my burdens with joy
and equanimity.
My acceptance shall sculpture a
     true form
for the Habitation of Spirit.

Deliver my soul, O Lord, from lying lips, and from
a deceitful tongue.
                                    —Psalm 120:2

Good
Guile
and the
Soul

Some are born to the world with an advanced or pure intuition. In childhood their naïvete is a marvel to behold. Should this rare quality be not bruised in the tender years, it will become, in mature years, the *good guile*. The good guile is a perceptive, non-intrusive sensitivity into the sensitivities of others.

When one has the grace to look into the thoughts and feelings of others without censure or judgment, he is the recipient of the confidence and trust of those who crave to be understood. All who are ordained to live close to the unseen moods and wounds of men have earned the grace of the good guile. Their words fall upon the ears of the weak as strength, wisdom, and peace.

The cunning mind can neither cope with nor comprehend the gratuitous benefits of the good guile. All should pray to unite themselves with the good guile. Consideration of others, the opening of the inner ear to the suffering and grief of others, the charitable word said when others would defame—this is the beginning of the good guile. One who has earned the good guile may direct and guide without offence.

*I shall work and hope and create.
God shall equate my motive and
    my honor.*

*

*I pray to use the good guile,
rather than the cunning mind.*

*

*I shall resound praises often.
In time, my pure words shall
    become the good guile,
speaking to the souls of men.*

Create in me a clean heart, O God; and renew a right spirit within me.
                                        —Psalm 51:10

Spiritual
Disciplines
When the portals of the heart are ajar, one cannot know condemnation or unforgiveness. He who offends the Good Law stands within that which disciplines him. His lessons are returned again and again until discipline is accepted by the heart and the mind.

One who accepts the spiritual disciplines opens the portals of his heart, and he communes with others who have opened the portals of their hearts and minds. And in his communing, his soul reveals that God separates not men, but unites them through Christ Jesus.

When the heart and the soul are one, they become as a golden urn filled with the fragrances of flowers upon the altar place of Heaven— fragrances which exude the essence of the purest light.

*I shall cleanse away the stubble
of the dying season.
I shall prepare my heart
for a new planting,
that grace may enter in.*

*

*I shall be satisfied only
when sense satiety
has become spiritual sensitivity.*

*

When I learn of the eternal
emanation
centered within all life,
I shall come nigh to reverence.

How much more shall the blood of Christ, who
through the eternal Spirit offered himself without
spot to God, purge your conscience from dead
works to serve the living God?

—Hebrews 9:14

I.
Conscience
and the
Soul

The past as experience is very precious indeed. The soul is the balancer between the past
and the present. One should trust in his soul to
evaluate and bring equilibrium to the aeons,
ages, epochs, and also to the former days of the
present life.

The power of the soul is enfeebled when one
continues to revive and sustain the anxieties
and frustrations of previous days, months, and
years. Responsible works of the present will
enable one to overcome irresponsible works of
the past.

When one has a contrite heart toward his
seemingly unresolved past actions, and discerns
that the sense-mistakes of the past may be recti-
fied through responsible acts and attitudes
within the very present, the soul enables him,
in right timing, to erase the accusing figments
of the past, and to hearken to the higher degrees
of a lucid conscience. In this, he will be reverently receptive to the guidance of his Guardian
Angel and Recording Angel. Thus, he will
receive the illuminative instruction relative to
the present, and will no longer linger upon
decaying deeds of the past.

*I shall command first my sense-
      indulgences,
and shall experience all things
through the pure, love-motive
      within.*

*

*May I be freed from exalted
      self-esteem.
May I know what I am,
      why I am;
and if my Guardian Angel will
      so permit,
may I know where I should go.*

*

*I expect not an easy hammock
      upon which to lie,
nor a mossy knoll upon which to sit.
May my endeavors be above and
      beyond
the sense-actions of the hours, days,
      months, years.
May my lucid thought
become united with the lucid
      conscience
waiting to tell me, to teach me.*

Pride goeth before destruction, and an haughty
spirit before a fall.
                                    —Proverbs 16:18

II.
Conscience   The physical body, the etheric body, the emotional body, and the mental body are seeking
to give a greater expression to the soul. He who
listens not to his conscience confines his soul,
and shuts it away; each body becomes a prison
house. And the world becomes a vacuum-like
place, in which he expresses not his soul.

One who has fallen into the state of emptiness
has not the way to reach his soul. He who wraps
himself in a flame of self-warming love is en-
raptured of himself and warms but himself.
However, he who burns away, one by one, the
self-egotistical shadows—and the layers of the
egotistical shell—prepares himself to stand in
the freeing light of his soul.

There can be no denying one's purpose, or his
ethic, or his uniqueness of expression and creation when the egotistical shell has been burned
away. Until the egotistical shell has been burned
away, obstacles will stand between man and his
true expression; and he will express something
of the biased or prejudiced, or he will produce
a genius which carries with it the means of
karma, or the wounding of other men in the
world.

Each day one should dedicate himself to the
overcoming of any selfish particles which ap-

pear in the mind, thoughts, and emotions. One should let the conscience turn the key to the greater powers of the soul. And even though one seems to work against the tide, the soul will give him the power to overcome.

*May my conceits
and my conscience
come to terms,
for I would speak
and know the true.*

*

*My soul-expression is of Heaven.
Somewhere in my human defeats
may be found the key
to my soul's expression.*

*

*In my spiritual covenant
I agreed to dissolve my egotistical
    shell.
I shall be neither surprised
nor dismayed
when change begins its sculpturing
    work.*

*

*I pray to overcome
stiffneckedness
and unteachableness.*

I said, Lord, be merciful unto me: heal my soul; for I have sinned against thee.

—Psalm 41:4

III.
Conscience   When the conscience is unclouded, the soul becomes a golden revealer. One is free to serve God when the conscience works as an approving asset rather than a reproving attribute.

The Saints of Heaven work unceasingly to purify the world-conscience. True prophets in the world sacrifice themselves to purify the conscience of nations and religions. The Recording Angel and Guardian Angel work to help each one to recover the purity of his intent and to dissolve the stains of imperfect and faulty works upon his record.

The service of a pure disciple meets no restraint when he has proven himself to his conscience. There are no barriers to the Eternal Grace supporting his work when the disciple fortifies himself with the approving asset of his conscience.

If it is Thy Will, provide me,
    O Lord,
with the good sense above sentience.
Multiply me, O Lord,
with Thy timely equation.
                    *

I will look firmly into my
    infirmities
and see the One Immutable
Affirming:

I am deathless, eternal;
God is the Will, the Life, the
  Light, the Love.

*

May the golden wonder
of childlike naïvete
take command of my incredulous
  mind
and make more supple my
  stubborn will.

Now the end of the commandment is charity out
of a pure heart, and of a good conscience, and of
faith unfeigned . . .

—I Timothy 1:5

Crisis
and the
Conscience

To love and to be loved is the desire of all persons. When the Love Fiat is abused, profaned, or denied, the conscience aspect of the soul, accompanying the Love Fiat, is obscured. Pure feeling being repressed, the thought and thinking become over-analytical or critical. Beneath this flaw-seeking and faultfinding lies the unresolved guilt related to the profaning of love.

The Love Fiat will not be denied. The conscience presses upon the heart in many and varied manners; for the conscience works as the fire of the soul to burn away and consume the selfish debris shading or veiling the soul's light.

The conscience is the admonitor for the soul. The soul-faculties are the clarifiers of the soul's intent. There enters into the life of each disciple an inevitable crisis period, in which the soul-faculties clarify and interpret what the conscience aspect of the soul would say.

Sometimes one enters into a dry spell or detachment from loving and being loved. Such dry spells are accompanied by self-criticism, and sharp criticism and analysis of others—as the capacity to love and to be loved seems to withdraw. A dry spell is usually followed by panic and a feeling of aloneness and loss. In this period of evolvement, the disciple himself becomes the subject or target of the criticisms of others. Even his smallest actions seem to come under the critical survey of many—and those near and dear become impenetrable and non-responding.

The Love Fiat seeks to speak through the conscience aspect of the soul, so that the disciple may love and be loved reverently, selflessly. When this period of initiation has spent itself, the disciple will open the portal of his heart to the Love Fiat, and he will be ready to act upon and to be guided by what the conscience would say.

Since I did ask for enlightenment,
I shall strive to behold
what is being disclosed by the
soul's light—
for the body filled with light
sustains the heart and mind with
joy and peace.

*

The immortal love within my soul
shall impart the sacred word
revealing my deathless sojourn
within the Eternal.

Why art thou cast down, O my soul? and why art thou disquieted in me? hope thou in God: for I shall yet praise him for the help of his countenance.

—Psalm 42:5

Conscience and the Soul's Medallion In the present scientific age, men are in the process of developing certain electronic machines to gauge, to estimate, and to define. While many of the aspects of life may be accelerated and also aided through such mechanical helps, no machine ever invented by man can replace or compare with the unfailing accuracy of the soul's equation.

All deviation from ethic is recorded upon the vibratory hum of the soul's medallion. All pain of the body, the emotions, and the mentality is caused by the discordance sounding upon this outer rim of the soul's medallion. The vibratory hum of the soul's medallion works unceasingly upon the conscience. Friction, tension, and unrest are caused by the magnified sounding of the vibratory hum.

Love is the peace winner; faith, the blessed sustainer; creation, the rhythmic organizer. These three channel and distribute the pressures banked upon the outer ring of the soul's medallion. When the heart's love, the pure imager within thought, and the soul's record are as one, the vibratory hum no longer resounds upon the conscience.

I give praise for my discontent;
for I know it to be the voice of
    my soul
reminding me to awake to the Real.

*

When my egotism or vanity
stands between my soul's light and
    grace,
I pray that I may face with
    courage
the Angel who holds the record of
    my faulty ways.

And now my soul is poured out upon me; the days
of affliction have taken hold upon me.

—Job 30:16

If ye endure chastening, God dealeth with you as
with sons; for what son is he whom the father chas-
teneth not?

—Hebrews 12:7

Conscience
and the
Vibratory
Hum

When the spiritual life is based upon the
Christ, one accepts the lessons of life as they are
given. The Guardian Angel times these lessons
to one as he needs them in his particular stage
of evolvement.

The vibratory hum of the soul is as a scorpion
in the conscience for some, as a chisel for some,
and as many hammers for others—reminding
them that rectification comes only through right
intent and right effort. When the vibratory hum
around the soul's medallion becomes heavily
burdened with wrong feeling, thinking and act-
ing, the conscience becomes as a fire, purifying
the thought and the mind.

He who accepts not his chastening has a bitter
spirit; and he sullies the waters upon which
the Spirit of God would move. Peace of mind
is earned through acceptance of chastening.
Right effort and acknowledgment of the greater
laws governing the conduct and attitudes of
men will, in time, result in illumination of
the mind.

*Let me not force anyone to do
what I would not do.*

Let me be not the accuser,
the avenger,
or the judge.
Time is my healer;
truth is my bulwark.

After those days, saith the Lord, I will put my law
in their inward parts, and write it in their hearts;
and will be their God, and they shall be my people.

—Jeremiah 31:33

Conscience
and the
Law
of God

The soul's medallion, the soul's record, and
the Guardian Angel of the soul determine when
one is ready to comprehend and accept the Laws
of God. When this occurs, the inward points of
light—the sacred atoms of man—are quickened.

The feeling of guilt and a weighted conscience are the results of extended deviation
from the Law of God. All men learn first the
rules, second the Ethic, and last the Law. It is
grace indeed when the Law of God is etched
into the mental attributes, into the heart, into
the actions.

A righteous man is one who is the governor
over many and ruler over none. It is world-
grace when ethical men are born to the world.

The spiritual seeker should often dwell upon
the love, justice, mercy, and equity of God;
for God has established the earth—and His
Law ordains, weighs, and equalizes.

In the Pro-Genesis Age there will be a great
majority of persons in the world who will have
absorbed the Law of God into their inward
parts. These persons will govern, manifest, and
create for God.

*Why should I dwell upon my
    frailties?
Am I not as strong
as the Law of God within me?*

*

*My trust is a lively compass
pointing truth-ward.*

*

*How lost would be an eternity
without law, justice.
So must I remember—
My world is governed since the
    beginning.*

*

*The Law of God knoweth neither
    rest,
sleep, nor season.
May my actions be pure;
for I would call upon the Law of
    the Lord
to sustain me, to support me.*

5

CREATION AND HEALING

For by him were all things created, that are in
heaven, and that are in earth, visible and invisible,
whether they be thrones, or dominions, or principali-
ties, or powers: all things were created by him, and
for him . . .
                                        —Colossians 1:16

**The Soul
and True
Creation**
True creation is greater than genius, for
genius is more often colored by the precocity of
egotism. True creation is a blended action of
perfected skills acquired from aeons of struggle,
ages of effort, and lengthy periods of humility
and reverence.

True creation appears in right timing and
delights the higher aspects of the senses, stimu-
lates the feelings, extends the desires, quickens
the soul's faculties, and stirs the germinal, creative power of thought. True creation is at one
with the powers of the soul and the soul-faculties. Such creation works in undisturbed unison
with the Rhythm of God.

Some of the barriers to creation are: self-
indulgence; lack of respect for the origin of
ideas; failure to express gratitude as to the source
of inspiration; failure to love work for work's

sake; failure to obey the training received from
the soul's voice or conscience; creating the ugly,
misshapen or malformed, so as to be different
or attract attention; failure to see God as the
true Creator of all; and failure to follow His
blueprint while creating.

The rhythm within emotions and thought will
duplicate the Rhythm of God when one begins
to free creation in the simple tasks or things
close by. These pertain to an inspired care of
the physical body; a selective sensitivity as to
association with persons; the perfect utilization
of time so as to make alignment with grace
timing; and the deliberate association with
objects of beauty.

The soul, at one with God, is a joyous soul—
and restrains not the one who would turn each
moment, action, emotion, or thought toward a
life of preciousness. Let the works of the disciple be creation. And let his moments become
monuments of immortality.

> *Let me recognize the tempter*
> *above the tempest.*
> *And let me not invite him to*
> *delay or stay with me.*
> *Let me still my lesser will*
> *and be at home with the angel*
> *who holds the sacred urn,*
> *anointing my brow with peace.*

*

I have opened the treasure house
of my soul.
I have found the sovereignty
of a greater power
than my lesser wishes or will.

Every good gift and every perfect gift is from above,
and cometh down from the Father of lights, with
whom is no variableness, neither shadow of turning.
—James 1:17

The Soul's Task

The soul's task is to urge one to create in this life, and to combine his creations with the creations of former lives. The soul's task is to inspire one to find the way to express his own uniqueness, and thus add to the wonderful spiritual prosperity in the world.

When the desire and the soul's task unite, one finds his true forte, or the manner in which he may create. When one dedicates his hands and heart, he comes closer to the expression of the soul's task.

There is a tremendous spontaneity to the soul's power once one has built a spiritual rhythm. This spontaneity will sometimes place upon one, almost overnight, a gift or a talent which comes as a soul task. In some cases, a gift or talent may appear in the latter years, for when one is younger he is more likely to listen to his senses rather than to his soul-faculties.

May I come into the creative side
of my soul,
and delight in the joy of creation.

*

My unrest is the product of my
aimlessness.

I pray to seek and to find
my soul's task.

*

My soul keeps me ever hopeful.
My dedication
sustains my cheerful knowing.
New designs and new ways of
*   beauty*
await my willing hands.

*

Each time I yield to depression
I come closer to self-destroying.
Each time I yield to joy
I am nigh to creation.

*

Through trial and error I learn.
Through desire for the true and
*   the beautiful,*
I am born to the unceasing ways
of creation.

Therefore whosoever heareth these sayings of mine,
and doeth them, I will liken him unto a wise man,
which built his house upon a rock . . .
                                    —St. Matthew 7:24

Character One should come to know the body's relation
to the soul. To attain this knowledge, he should
become aware of his personality. It is through
his character that he controls his personality
and all things affecting his body. Character is
the granite rock of the personality. Character
has been built from sacrificial works throughout the ages.

When there is strength of character in the
personality, one recognizes truth and follows it
with ethic. But he who has not character lacks
stamina. Without character, there is little peace.
When one has character, he listens to truth's
instruction, and becomes not a victim to ephem-
eral promises. When the personality is supported by character, one comes to peace; he
works with soul-construction, and becomes a
masterbuilder for God.

I pray for the strength
to act with courage,
regardless of how truth may affect
me or mine.

*

May I have the grace
to see with the eye single,

and to act without faltering
when the Holy Spirit moves me.

*

Each day I will ask myself,
"Has this day increased my
* spiritual stature?"*

*

For the thousands of tasks before me,
I draw upon the strength of the
* many*
who, having seen the Light,
have risen.

No man hath seen God at any time; the only be-
gotten Son, which is in the bosom of the Father,
he hath declared him.
                                    —St. John 1:18

**Worthi-
ness**   The "bosom of the Father" is that sacred
place of *heavenly vibrancy* where dwell the
Saints. Men must turn their faces again and
again to the bosom of the Father.

All men must prove their worth through
works of worthiness. When one has achieved
pure motive, works of worthiness begin, and the
golden road of happiness shall welcome the
joyous, worthy one. The golden road of happiness is built of golden deeds of worthiness. The
golden light of joy supreme is sustained by endless purifications and by works filled with spiritual fire.

Each man is single unto himself in his prov-
ing with God. But there comes a time in which
the many singles in their provings must combine,
and thus make up a holy nucleus in the bosom
of the Father and in the heart of God.

> *May my motives and my
>   conscience unite,
> and clarify the route
> for my works of worthiness.*
>   *
> *May the circumference of my
>   united self
> give freedom and perfect
>   fulfillment.*
>   *

Gold, frankincense, myrrh: Spirit,
  sacrifice, pain.
If these were the worthy gifts
  for Him,
I too shall receive them
with wisdom, love, joy!

Let nothing be done through strife or vain-glory;
but in lowliness of mind let each esteem other
better than themselves.

—Philippians 2:3

The Soul and the Ethic Constant turmoil within the emotions and thoughts restrains the pure ethic which would speak through the soul. The disciple should shun all feelings tinged with resentment and all thoughts inclined toward retaliation.

The soul will not obey the voice of cupidity, nor will it respond to harsh commands. The soul responds only to the cadence of the loving heartbeat set to the Rhythm of God.

The pure manifestations of the soul's true light are made possible when a selfless love, a continuing faith, a forgiving heart, and non-judging thought are sustained.

As long as physical work retains an over-emphasis as to physical rewards, the action of the physical world will produce aggressive works stimulated by the competitive standards in the world. One of the challenges confronting the disciple is the necessity to discern the difference between the spiritual ethic and standards expressed on the competitive levels of the physical world.

When the disciple has unwittingly compromised with a worldly, man-made standard, he will be diverted from his spiritual rhythm. In time, he will learn that he has been diverted because he has compromised and has upset the delicate balance between the ethic and manifestation.

The disciple will come to recognize all aggressive tumults which would try to divert him; and he will work to regain his spiritual poise and establish the ethic, so that he may avoid compromising with the temporal standards set by men in the world.

To obtain pure discrimination and the ethic necessary for the expression of a spiritual life requires many trials between the demands of man and the Commandments of God. Thus, the disciple should seek at all times to depend wholly upon the ethic as established in the Will of God, rather than to conform to the standards of men established solely for the convenience of men.

True dedication, sincerity of purpose, reverence toward all life, and love for one's work will produce an ethical approach to all facets of creation within the Plan of God.

> *I alone hold the key to inner*
> *harmony;*
> *for, if I will, my world*
> *shall become at one*
> *with the Will of God.*

Finally, brethren, whatsoever things are true, whatsoever things are honest, whatsoever things are just, whatsoever things are pure, whatsoever things are lovely, whatsoever things are of good report; if there be any virtue, and if there be any praise, think on these things.

—Philippians 4:8

Love, the Indestructible Reality

Love is the soul's ambassador. God's love is firmly implanted within the soul of each one in the earth. If one remains naive, pure, guileless in his love-desiring, his love will become as a soothing healer for the world.

When love is used as an instrument to wield the will of another, antagonism and even hate will result. The tuning fork of the soul, when free to expand through love, will give sensitivity and intuition as to love's action.

Response to the pure degrees of love is unfailing. If there be love motivated by acquiring, or if love be abused, the offender will receive unto himself a continuing scourge in the guise of love.

One should search his heart as to the cause of untender acts from others. He should seek to harmonize himself with the love theme of Heaven.

Spirit's skill—and the soul's tool—is a heart at one with the World of God. Let each one open his heart to the Love of God, and he shall love and be loved.

Pity the loveless, and love more; for love is

the creator, the selfless revelator, the restorer. Love is an indestructible reality, assuring immortality above and beyond the destructible.

My love and charity
will become as twin heart-streams,
flowing and giving—
equally, joyfully.

*

I shall master my fears with love.
My fears shall no longer veil
God's Will for me.

*

I am happiest when I love
selflessly.
I shall search my heart
and cleanse away my commands
of love
and my demands of love.

He that loveth his brother abideth in the light,
and there is none occasion of stumbling in him.

—I John 2:10

Love and the Soul   When the roots of love are implanted in healthy and virginal soil, the result is creation. One sustains the roots of love when he waters, feeds, and prunes the plant of love.

The soul of man will prompt him to dedicate his love in right timing, when his feelings are stirred by the hunger for love—pure love. Pure love activates the greatest of grace, and produces a sensitivity toward life.

There are four degrees of pure love: the love for Creation, the love for Life, the love for Light, the love for pure love. Pure love is that which loves Creation first, Life second, Light third, and love last.

He who lives sensuously loves love for love's sake. He who loves love for self shall see naught but the mirage of himself. He who loves Light shall be nurtured within the Light. He who loves the whole of Creation shall know his Creator—God.

If one works for the love of Creation, the love of Life, the love of Light, and the love of pure love, he shall have the impersonal love.

The Creation, the Life, the Light,
and the love within me shall
inspire me
to live completely for God.

*

I shall transcend my transgressions
by creating.

*

I shall transpose my trespasses
to life-giving and immortal works
through sincere action.

*

In the Light,
I shall overcome my errors,
with Truth as my prompter.

*

I shall heal and resolve my
        sorrows,
and set aright my morality
with pure love.

*

I shall look
and see beauty in everything.

*

I shall forgive
seventy times seven.

And at midnight there was a cry made, Behold, the
bridegroom cometh; go ye out to meet him.

—St. Matthew 25:6

The Soul's Tone

The years of one life are brief in the calendar of the Eternals. Each life has a soul tone and a spiritual theme. In each person there is an underlying hunger to unite the tone with the theme. Love is the voice of the soul's tone. Thought is the interpreter of the spiritual, creative theme. Creative, dynamic action results when emotion expresses the tone of the soul, and thought provides the spiritual theme.

Emotions are the first to change when one aspires to the spiritual life. The soul tone urgently directs the spiritual aspirant to cultivate the most tender aspects of love, to cherish the close affections, to revere the sacred intimacies, to enlarge the love-logos by speaking kindly, lovingly.

When the soul's tone and the spiritual theme are united through love's highest action and thought's purest expression, this is the true androgynous marriage alchemy. Emotion becomes the bride for the soul. Thought becomes the bridegroom for the Spirit.

Love is an immortal healer,
setting aright the bruises of the ages.
Divine love
is the elixir of life.

May my love
become as an endless river,
purifying, flowing, renewing.

Behold, I send an Angel before thee, to keep thee
in the way, and to bring thee into the place which
I have prepared.
                                    —Exodus 23:20

**Guardian
Angel
and the
Soul**

When one seeks a pure place for his Spirit,
his Guardian Angel and his soul will direct
him to an unsullied atmosphere. The unsullied
atmosphere is first built within; for if one is
sullied within, he cannot respond to an unsullied
atmosphere without.

Through ages, times and days, man regener-
ates himself. He overcomes and resurrects, until
he finds himself in a pure locale of the Spirit.

In the house of the soul, there are many spiritual windows waiting to be opened, waiting to
reveal a new vista onto the world without.
Cramped beliefs open not these windows of the
soul. If there be interior darkness within the
soul, the Spirit seeks to heal this darkness.
When man is healed of interior darkness, he
enters into the house of the soul. The windows
of the soul open, and he beholds the unsullied
atmosphere of his Spirit.

*The stillness of my Spirit
illumines my mind,
healing my heart wounds.*

*

*The immortal lily,
having its roots in mud,
gives me a comfort, a hope,*

and a reminder of my own risen
  grace.

*

Let me be pure without prudery.
Let me think purely without
  censure.
Let me love purely;
for where love is pure,
there is harmlessness.

> According to the grace of God which is given unto me, as a wise masterbuilder, I have laid the foundation, and another buildeth thereon. But let every man take heed how he buildeth thereupon.
>
> —I Corinthians 3:10

Self-Mastery and the Angels

The spiritual disciple is a heavenly apprentice, a ward of Heaven. His chief compass and director is the soul; his daily companions, the angels. Let the spiritual disciple become a perfect mirror for the Light. And let him learn self-mastery, that he may become a craftsman in the world of man.

The soul works incessantly to place the disciple in environments where he may gain self-mastery. Often, he may be placed where his works are little understood and appreciated, or he may be placed in positions of authority wherein he must yet prove himself (or be proven).

Wherever the disciple finds himself—if he be a truly devoted and dedicated disciple, and if he will keep in remembrance at all times that "the Father that dwelleth in me, he doeth the works"—he shall then receive honors in perfect timing as to his integrity grace; and he shall also become a veritable column or pillar of righteousness for God.

What my senses have fashioned,
my soul shall remedy.

*

I will root out my enemies within.
I refuse to house my enemies.
I shall cast them out one by one;
for I would build my foundation
upon the rock of God.

*

I shall assess my love
rather than my defeats.

*

If my cause be right, I cannot fail;
for the Angel of Righteousness
works within God's perfect
*   Equation.*

... To him that overcometh will I give to eat of
the hidden manna, and will give him a white stone,
and in the stone a new name written, which no
man knoweth saving he that receiveth it.

—Revelation 2:17

The Soul and the Stigmata

The stigmata are the pain antennas of the body. The stigmata are sensitive points in the lesser etheric body gained through the pain endured in sacrificial acts in former lives. Each disciple has some degree of stigmata sensitivity. The stigmata enable the disciple to remain in sympathy with the need of the world. Were it not for the stigmata sensitivity, the disciple would be opaque and blind to the suffering in the world; and he would become calloused and subjected to materialistic compromise. The stigmata are also the means through which the disciple drains off his own mental and emotional poisons.

The disciple becomes more sensitive than other persons because of the stigmata. When one is depleted in his healing works, he has in some manner offended the use of the stigmata. The disciple at all times should seek to translate the suffering of others into Light, and thus fulfill a selfless healing work. If he lingers overlong upon the thought of the grief or the pain that he prays to heal in others, he will irritate the stigmata, and he will find himself diverted from his path of effort.

The stigmata cannot function for anyone who has spiritual pride. Through the stigmata, the disciple is always in harmony with humbleness, giving, serving, reverence, charitableness, and the preserving of good. The stigmata keep the disciple continually aware of the sacrificial grace of the soul; therefore, he thinks less of himself and more of others.

> *My heart has loved throughout*
> *   the ages.*
> *My heart knows what is said*
> *of love in my heart.*
> *Let not my heart be faint.*
> *I shall love without restraint,*
> *and the response to my love*
> *shall be instant, quick!*

Then shall thy light break forth as the morning, and thine health shall spring forth speedily: and thy righteousness shall go before thee; the glory of the Lord shall be thy rereward.

—Isaiah 58:8

Healing Power of the Soul

Within the soul there is a stream of healing waters, flowing as an inward sea. In each illness there is the dewy rose of a dawn gathered from the promise of the soul's immortal healing power. When one arises to Light each day, he renews the immortal healing powers of the soul.

When the mind becomes as a clean page— and the thought transcribes the peace within the soul—healing comes. The immortal healing powers of the soul enable one to be charitable, pure, loving, and also enable one to understand the cause within sickness.

To receive of the immortal healing powers of the soul, one must open the inner ear, the inner eye. The innermost part of the medallion of the soul contains an immortal healing for mortal wounds. To receive of this immortal healing, one must still the insistent clamor of the senses.

When illness comes, the soul seeks to make union with the mind and the heart. There is an overflowing tranquility moving from the soul— far more powerful or dynamic than the senses registering pain.

When one is healed through the immortal powers of the soul, he has heard a higher tone

of the Spirit than that which is heard in the
sound of the senses.

*I shall move beyond the shallow
    reaches
of my senses
to the more profound depths
within my soul.*

*

*My soul contains
a diadem of remembrances,
of grace.
Whatever my senses say,
my soul knoweth more.*

For now we see through a glass, darkly; but then face to face: now I know in part; but then shall I know even as also I am known. And now abideth faith, hope, charity, these three; but the greatest of these is charity.

—I Corinthians 13:12,13

Charity and the Living Waters

When the rains are withheld from men, men suffer and know not why they suffer. When the downpourings from the Spiritual Worlds come not to men, men grieve and know not why they grieve. Yet, when the downpourings are with men, they look upon them as they look upon the natural waters of the earth and take them for granted.

There is a Source from which the rivers of life come. There are many outlets through which the rivers may flow. And there is an eternal way in which the waters of life are received. When one knows that the rivers of life come from God, the healing waters enter into his soul; the emotions are soothed, and the heart is healed. He who has charity seals in for all time the living waters of life which feed and nourish the ways of the soul.

May my charity
become an extension of love,
for I would be merciful,
loving.

*

I am weary of the walk in dry
places.

*May my feet lead me
to the "still waters."*

*

*The inner voice of my soul
reminds me to give praise,
for a new sound has been heard.*

*

*Listen to the Word,
O ministers of men;
for the Word would hold thee up
and build for thy soul
a worship place.*

Let him know, that he which converteth the sinner from the error of his way shall save a soul from death, and shall hide a multitude of sins.

—James 5:20

The Flame of Life

When the flame of life is tended with a careless hand, scarring imprints and deep wounds are made upon the vessel of the heart. When the flame of life is carefully nourished, it becomes a perpetual flame, and the soul will yield up its gifts of grace, of good.

Learn each day to think upon the flame of life. On arising in the morning hour, think upon the flame of life within the heart. Let it clarify the fears in the mind and burn away or consume the wrong turnings and wrong expectations.

The flame of life will overcome pain, and open the way for consummation grace. He who has received the consummation grace from the soul can hope for the Light.

The ministry of the good
is immortal;
the ministry of the pure
is eternal.

*

If my victory is for God,
it is well;
if it is for my will,
it doeth ill for men.

6

THE INITIATION OF THE HEART

By this shall all men know ye are my disciples, if ye have love one to another.
—St. John 13:35

The first requirement in discipleship is love. The disciple works to discipline his lesser will; to anticipate the love need of those near and by; to serve, not that he receive love as a reward for his actions, but rather that he be loving in all he does.

All of the records of non-loving are shadows upon the heart. Many come into the world insecure in their hearts, enamored only with their personal wills. Many come into the world encased in materialistic seeking, and seek only the sense outlet for the heart. Such persons are quick to cynically state that love is an illusion, a myth. However, the love emptiness in the heart is a very real experience in life or death. While all imbalance of the physical body is registered to the brain, all abuse of love is recorded deeply into the soul-sensitivity levels of the heart.

The heart is disciplined by the lack of loving, by the absence of being loved, and by the emptiness of being unlovable.

The seven steps in the initiation of the heart
as an organ of love are: Purification, Discipline,
Surrender, Love-Expression, Love-speaking,
Love-thinking, Love-creating.

The veils of pain and sacrifice
blend into the warming, healing
*   glow.*
I cease to fear.
I yield to peace,
to love.

He that overcometh, the same shall be clothed in
white raiment; and I will not blot out his name out
of the book of life, but I will confess his name
before my Father, and before his angels.

— Revelation 3:5

**Seven
Portals
Within
the Heart**
There are seven sacred portals within the
heart. One enters these seven heart portals one
by one. In this he works to attain the command
of the gravity action within the self-will.

To enter the first sacred portal of the heart,
one must undergo *self-denial*. To gain the second
sacred portal, he must achieve *self-control*. To
experience the third sacred portal, he must be
thoroughly aware of the necessity of *pure
emotion*.

To reach the fourth sacred portal, he must
increase his love-capacity to *selfless love*. To
reach the fifth sacred portal, he will have intuited God's love for him throughout many
lives, and thus he will have attained the *heart's
intuition* of love's intent. To reach the sixth
sacred portal, he must undergo the many
struggles, sorrows and griefs through every
earth circumstance—and not have lost his faith
or belief in God's power to help him to *overcome*
the visible and invisible adversaries. To reach
the seventh sacred portal, he must have experienced at first hand the knowledge of the *Everlasting Self*.

*I shall love, and analyze not
the why of my love;
for my heart must be free
of the bondage of fear.*

*

*Though the path often seems narrow
and the abyss deep,
I shall walk upward in my climb,
overcoming each obstacle;
for if I am to serve,
I must also partake of the strength
gathered from overcoming.*

Blessed are the pure in heart: for they shall see
God.
—St. Matthew 5:8

The Luminosity Atoms

There are four higher etheric atoms around the heart. These are called the *Luminosity Atoms*. When men harden their hearts and live within sensuality, these atoms are obscured; a veil-like or shadowy substance is formed between the heart and the soul. Thoughts and emotions are then channeled through the cunning will. Such men shut away the voice of the soul which would interpret to them the Will of God.

When the tremor of the lesser self is stilled within the heart of the disciple, the soul takes possession of its throne—the heart. And the Luminosity Atoms are free to reveal the true nature and purpose of man; for each Luminosity Atom carries a miniature, etheric, prototypal form of what man can be in the earth.

The Higher Self contains the image of what man has perfected in other eternities or world systems. The living-image within the sacred atom of the heart reveals what he is now. The Luminosity Atoms around the heart reveal what man can be in this eternity.

Contemplation or thoughts of holiness will bring freedom from the wrong acts which create tension and obstruct the voice of the soul. Meditation will expand the soul's capacity to free the blending process between the Higher Self, the living-image, and the Luminosity Atoms.

The voice of the soul is the revealer of life, for the soul holds the record of life. When the Luminosity Atoms around the heart are in alignment with the medallion of grace around the Higher Self, the voice of the soul will speak of the many lives of the past and of many lives to come. Only in the highest state of illumination may man behold the eternal life-rhythm as expressed through countless lives.

A look or a glance into my soul
is not enough;
for my heart would seek
wider horizons, broader vistas—
and I would stand in the grandeur
of my soul's sight.

*

If love is the ritual to free
what my soul would say,
then let love turn the sacred key.

Ye are the light of the world. A city which is set
on an hill cannot be hid.
                                    — St. Matthew 5:14

The Germinal Quality Within the Soul

In other eternities previous to this eternity, the Higher Self perfected the germinal quality within the soul. As many persons are yet to make alignment with their Higher Selves, so also are many in the world yet to make alignment with this germinal and illuminating quality within their souls.

The germinal quality within the soul is always at one with the eternal. This germinal quality gives to man the capacity to remember the works of other eternities and all of the actions and works of this eternity. The germinal quality within the soul sustains joy, praise, hope, faith. Many persons in the world are unaware of the germinal quality within the soul; their temporal beliefs short-circuit or seal away that which would speak to them of the everlasting, immortal and eternal. Men who love with undying love are inheritors of eternal life. Such men become the Elect; and their actions survive and are sustained over the aeons and the ages.

The germinal quality within the soul retains and keeps alive the embodiment record from life to life; absorbs and records the record of each day's good actions, and rejects the negative record so that it might be imprinted upon the vibratory hum; enables the one dying to read his life-record at death; and inspires the need to return to the physical world to balance the unresolved actions of former lives.

At the end of each day during dusk, the germinal quality within the soul extracts the good as grace and rejects the non-good—the non-good becoming the unfinished works, or the task for tomorrow and for other tomorrows in evolvement. However, the germinal quality has a healing action. Were it not for this, man would remain calloused, hard, opaque. Through repeated loving and reverent actions, the thought, the emotions, and the will shall, in time, come into harmonious alignment with the germinal quality within the soul.

No thing, nor any one, has a
mortgage on my soul,
or possesses me, save I consent.
If there be claims,
let my soul instruct me
as to right timing and right balance.

*

What shall fan the flame of my
soul's action:
love, or works, or truth?
I shall agree,
and begin to do that asked of me,
sacredly, happily.

Then said Jesus, Father, forgive them for they know
not what they do. And they parted his raiment and
cast lots.
                                                —St. Luke 23:34

The Remedial Power of the Soul

The remedial power of the soul is activated by the Life Fiat within our Father's forgiving love. To free the remedial power of the soul, the disciple seeks to forgive all trespasses coloring the lives of the past and of now. He discerns in the wrong acts of others the reflection of his own former actions; thus, in forgiving the acts of others, he forgives himself. The remedial power of the soul begins the cleansing, healing, and miraculous works—and all obstructions shading the soul's light are gradually resolved.

There is a forgiving magnanimity within a childlike heart. All disciples should seek to acquire this. Hate and distrust are scourgers, preventing the heart's alignment with the soul. The first heart-logos is forgiving love. The first thought-logos is the charitable mind. When thoughts of retaliation, hate, condemnation, or judgment cloud the mind, the remedial power of the soul is restrained in the healing work of peace sustaining. As long as one small shadow of unforgiving in feeling or thought shades the soul's light, the remedial power of the soul remains inactive.

One dedicated, forgiving person becomes a living catalyst to society, setting up a creative cycle of unending remedial works in the world.

The remedial power of the soul offers an unobstructed alignment with the grace of the soul, providing communion with the intelligible degree of thought which elucidates all actions and their portent. Thus, the soul's remedial power will reveal the cause within karma, and this illuminative experience will produce an absolute healing action. Faith in the remedial power of the soul illumines the thought; the sacred atoms come into alignment. Healing with wisdom speaks to him who believes on the miraculous powers of the soul.

*Through the many ages my soul
has carefully, patiently,
lighted my way.
I shall trust, believe, know and
experience
the immortal word of my soul.*

*

*I shall accept
the result of my soul's remedial
action.*

We have also a more sure word of prophecy; where-
unto ye do well that ye take heed, as unto a light
that shineth in a dark place, until the day dawn,
and the day star arise in your hearts . . .
                                          —II Peter 1:19

**The
Chalice
of the
Heart**

The Chalice of the heart is a protective etheric covering around the area of the heart's action. This etheric covering receives the imprint of desire, motive, intent, conscience. When the heart has fulfilled its complete expression as to pure love, the heart will center itself in the Chalice. The Chalice of the heart will eventually correlate to the true Christ Chalice symbolic of sacrifice and of resurrected life.

The Reverence Flame, the Truth Flame, and the Wisdom Flame of the heart, moving against the etheric covering around the organ of the heart, determine what action there is in the Chalice. The Chalice of the heart has three levels: the *Fiery Chalice* which relates to the senses; the *Golden Chalice* which relates to the soul; and the *Rainbow Chalice* which relates to the Higher Self.

The *Fiery Chalice* is the product of the sentient atoms' action. When a person lives sensuously in actions, feelings or thoughts, the etheric covering around the heart is aflame with the fiery flame of sentience, and the three Flames of the heart build a fiery wall around the living-image within the heart. One's conscience, rather than working through reason or logic, presses against the living-image within the heart—producing pain, remorse, regret. The Reverence, Truth, and Wisdom Flames of the heart become the reprovers of his actions, and the heart is the recipient of his karma.

The *Golden Chalice* is formed when the soul and the thought are in pure alignment. The heart is the organ of love, courage, fortitude. The Golden Chalice of the heart is built out of the ages of trial, transgression, endurance, overcoming, and hope. Through reverence, the Fiery Chalice may become the Golden Chalice. Through truth, the Golden Chalice may become the Rainbow Chalice—and the Rainbow Chalice will express the Wisdom Flame speaking for the Will in God.

The *Rainbow Chalice* is formed when the heart, the soul, and the Higher Self are in alignment. The Rainbow Chalice of the heart is the cup overflowing with the grace of pure love's striving and fulfilling throughout the ages. Only those who love selflessly have formed the Rainbow Chalice. The greater Chalice of the heart is called the Rainbow Chalice because the colors given off from the Luminosity Atoms around the heart, when seen with the inner eye, resemble the rainbow's glow.

Those who have formed the Rainbow Chalice of the heart are communicable to all peoples in the world. They possess the vowel of the world-logos—and, in their love-speaking, all languages and barriers are open. Such persons are the ambassadors who heal and serve, give and forgive. These are the saints-to-be, for the Rainbow Chalice of the heart is the sacred urn of the saints, who anoint, heal, and serve in love.

When the disciple fills this Cup or Chalice of the heart to overflowing, he is at one with the Lord of Love. He then becomes a heart-disciple who has mastered the little will which would stand between him and his walk on the Way. The Rainbow Chalice of the heart is built out of countless sacrifices through the ages, in which love has become selfless. From this selflessness comes the valiant strength to withstand the trials in discipleship.

Those who love selfishly suffer heartbreak, as they love without wisdom. Those who harden their hearts to the Real suffer heartache, as they have deadened their ears to the truth of the Real. An empty heart devoid of love is incapable of heartache. And he who has an unbelieving or non-trusting heart is one who lacks reverence in each thing, and gives not the all of himself. When there is a continued sense of awareness of the heart as the center of unfulfilled desire, the egotistical shell standing between the person and the Rainbow Chalice begins its dissolving.

In the disciple's life each initiation is accompanied by a heart-trial. This may be one of seven heart-trials: (1) unrequited love; (2) loving a person who is loveless; (3) loving for return of love; (4) believing not on love; (5) loving the self; (6) being loveless; (7) loving. The disciple reflects each of these heart-trials in some manner throughout many lives. In every disciple's life one of these heart-trials may be emphasized. When the disciple reaches the last heart-trial—when he is loving—he knows then that a loveless heart creates an empty life without meaning.

The key to unlock the long sealed
*   mystery*
lies at hand—
only one step more of love's
*   overflowing grace.*
I enter in and stand.

For the Lord God is a sun and shield: the Lord will
give grace and glory: no good thing will he withhold
from them that walk uprightly.
—Psalm 84:11

Pulsation of the Soul

Upon completion of the heart initiations, one opens the door between the soul and the living image within the heart; the higher degrees of soul-grace move gently forth to blend and mingle softly with what has transpired in the love sustaining. The disciple may compare this occurrence to that of hearing music beyond the range of the physical ear—music which blends with the heart's warming glow. The soul sounds the Tone speaking of the Will, the Life, the Light, and the Love of God.

The soul is not encased in a form. The soul's action is similar to a great pulsation, in that it moves in expansion and contraction. When the soul's power, life, light, and love are freed through a pure heart intent, the soul will expand forth to color one's thought with sacred thoughts inherent in God.

The soul is immortal and eternal. Man entered this world centered in his soul's power, life, light, and love. The disciple seeks to free and release the expanding capacity of the soul. The soul spiritually commands all pulsation of the physical body, such as the heartbeat, the pulse in the body. The atoms of the four bodies are continually seeking to coordinate with the soul's pulsation.

The word "soul" comes from sol or sun. In the first great intervals of this earth's creation— as man moved through the moving deep, and while the sun was yet in a nebular state—the Eternal Sustaining Atom, the Higher Self, and the soul received their quickening for the earth's work.

Man is a living soul, with an everlasting body. The soul is the breath of the everlasting body. The pulsation of the soul is the heartbeat of the everlasting body. Even as the yeast works in the loaf, so does the soul work to send forth its expanding action, speaking its logos of that which God would have man hear, see, and speak.

More than my heart,
more than my thought,
my soul Knows.

For ye were as sheep going astray; but are now returned unto the Shepherd and Bishop of your souls.
—I Peter 2:25

The Shepherd of the Soul

The Lord Jesus is the Shepherd of the soul
and the heart. When one ignores the love-
emanation of his soul, or when he refuses to
love with magnanimity, he obeys not the Shepherd of his soul and heart.

Persons who love not, have fearful hearts.
When the soul, the mind, and the heart work
separately rather than as one, a person is isolated, desolate. He who obeys not the good
Shepherd of the soul and heart has an untruth-
ful mind; a mind filled with fallacies; a mind
of wrong resolvings and concludings. All who
would live in peace with themselves should
seek to be at one with the Shepherd of the soul
and heart, and follow Him.

Love is an irresistible power
healing my wounds
and overwhelming my adversaries.

7

THOUGHT AND WILL

Then said Jesus unto his disciples, If any man will come after me, let him deny himself, and take up his cross, and follow me. For whosoever will save his life shall lose it: and whosoever will lose his life for my sake shall find it. For what is a man profited, if he shall gain the whole world, and lose his own soul? For the Son of man shall come in the glory of his Father with his angels; and then he shall reward every man according to his works.

—St. Matthew 16:24-27

Liberty

The desire for liberation, freedom, and detachment is innate in all men. To gain freedom of mind and of emotions, one must become free of self-restraints imposed upon him by erroneous thinking and feeling. To obtain liberty, one must give liberty to others; he must also learn to view the rights of others with liberation and charitableness.

In spiritual evolvement, with frequent renewals gathered from the soul's prompting, one achieves a holy detachment toward goals, objects, conditions, or situations. True freedom and liberty are experienced when one sees that liberty and freedom come only when one *loses* himself that he may gain the whole and the all.

168

All of the freedom I have today
is the result of my releasing-love
in the past.
I give thanks
that I may choose, learn,
and also release with love.

For if there be first a willing mind, it is accepted according to that a man hath, and not according to that he hath not.
                                    —2 Corinthians 8:12

Wherefore gird up the loins of your mind, be sober, and hope to the end for the grace that is to be brought unto you at the revelation of Jesus Christ.
                                    —I Peter 1:13

The
Higher
Intellect   When one is concerned wholly with the physical world, he shuts away the higher attributes of thought. His soul is as a bird caged; his soul cannot spread its light. This causes mental suffering. Only in the freeing of the outgoing and incoming light of the soul may one be free.

He who expands his soul's light frees his creation, his talents—and becomes self-disciplined, balanced, orderly, ruly, consistent, harmonious, fragrant, tender, kind, beautiful. When this occurs, the soul has an equalized polarity in all of the functions of the body and mind.

Dedication, prayer, contemplation, and meditation enable the soul to expand its light.

He who fears to give his soul the free play of his higher intellect will be deceived or fall into the hands of deceptive persons. He who fears cannot use his soul's light. He who has a fearful heart cannot use his soul's love.

Give to thy emotions love, if thou wouldst give to thy soul its true range. Give to thy mind an open intellect, an intellect of attentive-

ness and interest, if thou wouldst give thy soul
its free play.

The admonitor of my soul
will show me the true,
and will caution me of the untrue.

*

While I know I am different,
let me think not of myself as an
exception, or exceptional.
Only what I really *am will remain*
the same
throughout this eternity.

*

The bounteous way requires
an eager and perfect stewardship.
Let me become a better steward
of bountifulness.

> Enter ye in at the strait gate: for wide is the gate,
> and broad is the way, that leadeth to destruction,
> and many there be which go in thereat: Because
> strait is the gate, and narrow is the way, which
> leadeth unto life, and few there be that find it.
>
> —St. Matthew 7:13,14

Teaching with the Heart

To teach with the intellect without love offends those who love. To teach with intellect will cause him who thinks with intellect to defend what he has gathered in his concepts. The intellectual teacher reaps perishable fruits. He who teaches to the intellect receives nothing but the mirroring of his own egotistical shell. That which works through egotism cannot be for Heaven. He who would follow the straight way of the soul overcomes the egotistical shell. When one teaches with his heart, he follows the straight way of the soul. Having taken himself in hand, he is ready to follow the Will of God.

Three things which cannot be hidden in the world are egotism, selfishness, and a crooked heart. These things speak loudly in their clamor. Egotistical men are, by natural order, selfish and ill-motivated. These things do exist in the world—and he who would lead others must contend with these existing conditions.

When courage is as a pure flame, it will irritate the one who is ill-motivated, causing resentments and revilings. He who would teach others and lead others must lead with courage, and must doubt not himself or his capacity to lead.

When thou art authority, be authority not for authority's sake, but be authority in that thou workest with the law which hath been made plain to thee in thy heart and in thy mind. When the law hath been made plain, thou becomest a projection of the law, and thus the law in thee is unto God rather than unto thyself.

May pride and vanity
be dislodged from my personality,
for they are hindrances
to my soul.

*

Let me know not self-pity when I
*   am accused.*
Who can hide my good or name
*   my fault,*
save Him who is Just, True.

*

The good I have done needs no
*   acclaim.*
The good I will do,
I will do for the love of good.

*

Only a forgiving heart may ignite
and burn away the egotistical shell.

When wisdom entereth into thine heart, and knowledge is pleasant unto thy soul; Discretion shall preserve thee, understanding shall keep thee . . .

—Proverbs 2:10,11

Though I speak with the tongues of men and of angels, and have not charity, I am become as sounding brass, or a tinkling cymbal.

—I Corinthians 13:1

Freedom from Egotism

He who is all intellect is partial. He who is all sentiment is biased. When the intellect and the heart blend, true charity begins—and one enters into the living waters of the soul. When one works with the living waters of the soul, he works with true charity. He seeks not to compromise or appease; he seeks to give ease and to heal the griefs caused by the imperfect works in the world. He carries a lamp which is blown not out by the winds of egotism. The calm of his spirit is balm for the weary.

Let the intellect be devoid of egotism, and the heart be above sentient sentiment. For God loves a goodly craftsman—a worker who doeth good with a pure heart and an undefiled thought. The perfect love of God may do its perfect work when the impartial mind and the charitable heart unite.

I know that egotism
often disguises itself
through self-preservation.

*I pray to know a true humility
devoid of self-praise.*

*

*The Host or Hierarchy and my
     Guardian Angel
preserve my individuality.
May I revere the selfhood
in all men.*

*

*Since I entered into true charity,
I have found the blessed humility.
My love forgives, and my thoughts
     are rich
within the creative world of God.*

*

*I am continually amazed
and constantly astounded
by that which makes men so
     different,
yet so allied
through a common theme
of inspiration.*

The words of wise men are heard in quiet more
than the cry of him that ruleth among fools.
—Ecclesiastes 9:17

Be still, and know that I am God . . .
—Psalm 46:10

Quiescence The greatest of the spiritual arts is *quiescence*.
When the soul is at rest within Divine Spirit,
the mediative powers of Divine Spirit, or the
works of the Christ, begin. When one is agitated
as to the senses, his thoughts are as shallow little
boats caught in a storm; he is without aim or
purpose, and defeats Heaven's intent for him.

The Christ or Divine Spirit is as a magnet
drawing all pure thoughts upward into varied
prisms of Light. Inevitably, pure thoughts are
complemented and reinforced by correlated
spiritual powers received through mediation.
Regardless of trial or stress, when one seeks to
reach quiescence or an undisturbed repose in
thought, he will extend his degree of divinity;
and he will learn to meditate with a reverent
anticipation of the Divine interplay among all
beings expressing Divine Spirit.

The quiet, the blessed quiet,
shall free me, heal me.
I shall look upward
toward Light and more Light.
*

All beginnings are at one
within the Soundless Sound.

*Let my soul's voice be the tongue
for Soundless Sound.*

*

*I pray that Divine Spirit
shall be glorified within my thought,
and magnified through pure works.*

Unto thee, O Lord, do I lift up my soul.

—Psalm 25:1

Thought and Spirit The soul is the mediator between thought and Spirit. One should rely upon his soul to expand his thought patterns, and thus free the higher mind.

It is folly to scatter one's thoughts or to think with vanity. One should avoid mental arguments and dissensions.

When one conserves the vitality within his thinking, his thought will reach a state of Knowing or Niscience. The good justice within the Equation of God shall then give equanimity and peace to his thoughts. He should wait upon his soul to reveal the perfected ideas of Spirit residing within the Christ Mind.

I shall think on perfect justice
rather than justification.

*

My wishful thinking
shall no longer obscure the greater
ideas of God
waiting to speak through me.

*

If fear has made me cowardly in
my thinking,
I shall think courageously, nobly—
and God's Intelligible Spirit
shall enter into my mind.

In the multitude of my thoughts within me thy comforts delight my soul.
                              —Psalm 94:19

Clarifying the Mentality   In the World of Light, there are ideas which are yet to come to the earth. In the world of mind, there are faculties yet unripened. In the world of desire, there are yet unknown desires. Thus, confusion plagues the mentality of man.

When the soul clarifies the mentality and the desires, the mind then functions within the World of Light, where dwell the greater ideas of God.

The light of the soul releases the spiritual power within the mind and the emotions. Spiritual power proceeding from the light of the soul is accompanied by the angels. Into the mind and emotions enter wisdom, gentleness, tenderness. When one is powerful with gentleness, the angels' wings fan the flame of truth— and he speaks truth fearlessly to the world.

> *O angels, thou art at home in*
> *   Heaven;*
> *come nigh unto me*
> *with thy luminous,*
> *lifting ways.*
>   *

> *May I receive*
> *the holy transfusions*
> *between angel and man.*
>   *

*The saints stand nigh
unto God's Way and Word.
The angels dwell nigh and by His
    throne.
Let me know the reality
of His Kingdom in my domain.*

*

*My news shall be as a spreading fire,
dispersing the obstructions
built by unknowing men.*

*

*Let the holiness of Heaven
enter into my reason.
Let me receive the Light
into my mind and my heart.*

In your patience possess ye your souls.

—St. Luke 21:19

Eternal
Patience

Pity the one who knows not the difference between brass and gold; or the one who knows not the difference between the bitter cup and the sweet; or the one who plants his seeds in corruption. Pity his harvest on the morn.

When one has eternal patience, he will see that those who reap from faulty trees bring forth faulty fruits.

When one's virtues are unblemished, this will be written as grace on his record for the day. When one's virtues are unblemished, he may say at the end of each day, "I have done as well as I may in Christ. Let the Light search me; and let me know that I did aspire on this day to do that which my soul would say."

When thoughts linger on self alone,
the angels veil their nearness,
and the works of God
are unrevealed.

*

I seek the pathway
of holy discrimination.

*

Faulty judgments weigh heavily
upon my mind and heart.
I can arise only as high
as my trust.

*

*The springs of pure, healing waters
are healing freshets for my wounds.
May I be healed of selfishness.*

O keep my soul, and deliver me: let me not be
ashamed; for I put my trust in thee. Let integrity
and uprightness preserve me; for I wait on thee.
—Psalm 25:20,21

The Seven Thought Impulses

There are seven thought impulses. The four lower thought impulses are subtle-subversive, suggestive, retrogressive, and alienative-destructive. The three higher impulses of thought are illuminative, revelatory, and creative. When one has overcome the four restless, disquieting, and lower impulses of his thinking, his soul enables him to rise above the alternating pendulum of thought.

Through absolute faith in God, through being wholly at one with the Will of God, one forms a soul-shield of insulation. His thoughts rest upon a coherent, lucid field. Creating with God, he receives the *third vitality,* whereby his mental capacities are expanded. His actions appear phenomenal to those who yet must arise above the pendulum trials of alternating thought or thinking.

> *Let me adhere to the rules without
> resentment.*
> *Let me accept disciplines with
> understanding.*
> *Let me look not for the prize
> without effort.*
> *Let me rejoice in my ever-changing
> changelessness.*
>
> *

*I shall begin
each day
to keep a high tryst
with my thoughts.*

*

*I shall wear
my responsibilities
as a crown.
From the good responsibles
I shall learn.*

Truly my soul waiteth upon God: from him cometh
my salvation.
                                    —Psalm 62.1

**Response
to the
Soul Tides** The soul is as a great sea with incoming and
outgoing tides. The mind is as a golden meshed
net. Thoughts are as fish, great and small. Small
irrelevant thoughts move in and out of the
golden mesh of the mind. The incoming tides
of the soul vitalize and quicken the verities
fixed within the golden mesh of the mind.

One is inspired to do immortal things when
he responds to the incoming soul tide. He is
renewed; his vision is illumined; he is stirred
to create, to fulfill.

When the soul tide is low, one feels strangely
desolate, forsaken; he often yields to delinquent
ways. When one is aware of the importance of
the soul tides in his spiritual life, in selfless
industry he utilizes the dry times, and thus prepares himself for the incoming tide of his soul.

When one is in a state of grace, the soul tides
are quickened; thought becomes revelatory;
actions become works of holy providence.

*May I adhere to the ethic,
so that I may receive of the verities,
for I would work with a quickened
        perception
within the Eternal Will.*

*I pray for the grace to remember,
to utilize the incoming
lighted thoughts.*

For thou wilt light my candle: the Lord my God
will enlighten my darkness.
—Psalm 18:28

**The
Dynamic
Power
of the
Soul**

The disciple intuits how very close he is to
his soul. Were it not for the dynamic power of
the soul, coloring and influencing his thoughts,
all of his thinking would be sentiently concerned. Pure thoughts enable one to have access
to the Higher Worlds. When thoughts are pure,
the soul works in conjunction with the Kingdom of Heaven. Thought becomes dynamic
when pure ethics are observed in thinking. To
think of others with trust, to avoid labeling or
classifying those brought to one's attention in
daily life, enables the soul to become the clari-
fier of the thinking as to persons and events.

The dynamic power of the soul helps the disciple to receive telepathic instruction from the
soul. This level of telepathy becomes the prompter—correcting and balancing the thought. The
disciple has begun his spiritual evolvement
when he is aware of the continual correcting
and prompting of his soul. Thus, as the disciple
becomes more lucid in his thinking, he begins
to make more meaningful his world. To ignore
the telepathic prompting of the soul is to upset
the equilibrium of the individuality and the
equanimity of the mind.

The saintly personages in the Kingdom of
Heaven work unceasingly to make holy the

thoughts of those who have good intent, yet lack the strength to sustain pure thought. The disciple is fortified in the knowledge that the power of mediation will increase his capacity to think dynamically. And eventually he will become qualified to receive telepathy from the Christ Mind. Let the disciple listen to the dynamic power of the soul within his thought, and he will fulfill the Plan for him.

All of the lasting actions,
since the beginning of this eternity,
began with pure thinking.
I shall gather my harvest of
intelligence,
and I shall rhythmically
order my thoughts.

But as many as received him, to them gave he
power to become the sons of God, even to them
that believe on his name:
                                    —St. John 1:12

**Powers
of the
Soul**

God enables those who offend the laws of the
mineral, plant, or animal kingdoms to *transpose*
their transgressions into humane works and acts.
He also provides that one may *translate* every
trespass by taking unto himself burdens centered
within the family environment and placement.
And, finally, He makes it possible for each one
to *transform* his sinful deeds into works of good.

The powers of the soul begin their enlargement and magnification when one acknowledges
his transgressions, trespasses, and sins.

When one's intent is pure, and sincere, the
Recording Angel will provide the sustaining
power; the soul will reveal the way of trans-
posing, translating, and transforming; and the
Guardian Angel will time each event, making
it possible for such ones to become renewed
vessels for God.

*The love of my heart
shall warm and illumine my mind.
And I shall behold
the law of perfect justice.*

*

*I am centered within a universe
of unceasing creation,
a world of continuing action.*

*I am supported
by the verity of God.*

*

*May my soul become as a goodly
    sifter;
for I would retain
the beauty of introspective quiet
while in blessed unison with my soul.*

*

*The ascended arc
is the rainbow symbol of mediative
    harmony.
May I blend with each perfect
    prism,
and become at one
with the many facets of the
    Perfect Self.*

> . . . I humbled my soul with fasting; and my
> prayer returned into mine own bosom.
>
> —Psalm 35:13

Authority   There are few mighty mortal men. God gives authority to those who love Him, and who know the true authority to be the Law of God and the Will of God. He who names himself as an authority walks toward brambles and pitfalls, for he has a mind filled with fantasies and a will centered in self-delights.

One earns authority by first cleansing away the small, petty things, even as he would sweep away irritating fragments which make unsightly his house. When one believes on the greatness of his soul, rather than on the greatness of his personal self, he will unite himself with the greatness in the souls of immortal men.

> *My good is my soul-mantle of*
>   *grace.*
> *Let me continue in good ways,*
> *for I would be free of envy*
> *when I contemplate*
> *the great ways of noble men.*
>
>   *
>
> *Jesus asked,*
> *"Why callest thou me good?"*
> *For He knew that men*
> *understood not the source of good.*

Let me remember the Father
as the source of good
in all men.

*

For each tender thing done unto me,
I give thanks.
For each act of mercy
covering my awkwardness,
I give praise.

*

If there be appearance of evil,
May my good angel redirect
my feet.

Oh that men would praise the Lord for his goodness, and for his wonderful works to the children
of men! For he satisfieth the longing soul, and
filleth the hungry soul with goodness.

—Psalm 107:8,9

**The
Selfless
Will**   Flowing peace and the rhythmic harmony
from the soul's stream must come by the invi-
tation of the will. When the will is selfless,
devoid of caustic passion and free of self-made
agony, then the soul can speak in its stream,
and flow through the mood of man into his
mind. Into all processes of his creation shall
come peace and order.

Pure spirit and the soul's light have not
quenching. Deception, greed, and sordidness
shut away the soul. All of the things which man
would do to profane himself, he does against
his soul. Let thy soul-faculties move in thy soul
with freedom. Lose not sight of the freedom of
thy soul. Lose not sight of what thy soul saith
to thee.

*The wind and storm have had
their way with me.
I am fired and cleansed.*

*

*My love and my prayers
draw me nigh to God.*

My mouth shall speak of wisdom; and the meditation of my heart shall be of understanding.

—Psalm 49:3

To Become a Personage When one reaches a mature decision, he brings his grace into focus, and his destiny begins to be colored by happenings of ultimate good. Mature decisions bring him closer to his soul.

The soul's purpose is to inspire one to become a personage rather than a personality. A personality seeks to be spirited; a personage seeks to be spiritual. A personage leaves his mark upon the world; a personality indents his presence upon the world through particularizing eccentricities.

In the spiritual life, the soul is the supreme influence. One should know more of the soul's influence, and thus become a personage. When one is exposed to a personage, his grace is stirred—and each small thing said is engraved into the mind, whereby in future times it may become a tangible reminder of truths believed on and adhered to.

My lucid mercies,
rather than my indulgences,
are as a rock
unto my soul's foundation.

*

God has His ambassadors of good.
I pray to be without judgment,
for good is nullified by judgments.

I have longed for thy salvation, O Lord; and thy
law is my delight. Let my soul live, and it shall
praise thee; and let thy judgments help me.

—Psalm 119:174,175

The Law of God   When one saith, "How fabulous!" let him
return to the Law, which saith, "More than
fabulous is God, more than wondrous is He!"
Then shall he begin to seek not excitements or
the glamor way. He shall enter into the Reality
of God; and he shall come to assess the "fabulous" as false for him.

He who spends the wonder-naïvete of his soul
upon the fabulous shall fall into mental magics.
His imaging powers shall become an untrust-
worthy mirror, leading him to by-ways and
waste-ways. The untrained credulity will make
him an exploiter rather than a discoverer.

Through obedience to the Laws of God one
returns to the wonder-naïvete of the soul; and
he shall become a discoverer of God and for
God. He shall see in all things the testimony
of the Will of God, the Power of God, the
Might of God.

*May the Angel of my Day
protect me from the snares
awaiting my imprudent hopes and
works.*

*

*I shall climb a small hill each day.
How else may I gain an overlook
to behold tomorrow's plan?*

*

*I know harmony comes from many
        actions,
emotions, and thoughts
repeated in countless perfect works.
I pray for harmony
before I tell others
what I am, what I feel, what
        I think.*

Of his own will begat he us with the word of truth, that we should be a kind of firstfruits of his creatures.
—James 1:18

Pure Individuality

The soul works without ceasing to protect the very special uniqueness in each one. The soul patiently works with each person—through ages of emotions and thoughts—to produce outstanding and distinguishing characteristics and virtues.

There are many priceless ingredients and essences in the make-up of the individuality. Each person should learn to cherish his individuality as a priceless gift, and should resist any deviation seeking to thwart the uniqueness of the individuality or the "I".

In the spiritual life, one is asked to learn how to remain the "I" without egotism, how to remain singular without false humility. These are possible when one turns toward the greatest Individual of the earth—Jesus.

*My works now become joyous
with holy enthusiasm;
and, if it is the Will,
I would partake of the saintly
communion
accompanying works of worthiness.*

*

*May I learn to relinquish
with graciousness,
and see the unending compensations
of God's renewing and giving to
the world.*

> Justice and judgment are the habitation of thy
> throne; mercy and truth shall go before thy face.
> —Psalm 89:14

Spiritual
Power
and
Authority

It is often stated and believed that some persons are more blessed than others. However, when the work of the soul's medallion is truly discerned, the greater Laws of God can be seen as undeviating and impartial—for justice is meted out to each and all in right timing as to need and assimilation. When soul-grace produces some special prize or seems to show some favor as to talent, position, and happiness, this is the result of a person's effort, struggle, and pure actions in former lives—and reveals the Justice and Love of God.

To sustain the good requires a reverent and grateful heart, and also necessitates the using of grace in continued good works and healing works. Such soul-grace is divinely contagious, and stirs the heart atoms of all who are near this sacred and holy atmosphere. The right use of grace produces spiritual power and authority, and offers one an uninterrupted opportunity through which to serve. The mighty stature of the soul's power, using the law of right placement and timing, never varies as to the catalyst action in answer to the need of persons, conditions, and environment.

The disciple's day-by-day works of good, combined with the grace of his soul, give him the right to use the higher authority extended from the grace of the Higher Self. When such grace is manifested in continuous action, the disciple may receive the spiritual gift of authority over malignant conditions and chronic diseases—and the power to use the little-known, miraculous healing of the impossible and the improbable comes forth to inspire and give comfort to the world. All disciples should work toward earning these higher aspects of grace. Continuing actions of pure intent, with faith sustaining the works of immortal good, will result in the true authority as used by the Lord Jesus.

*I am no longer fearful of injustices
    and oppressions,
for I know the true—
and I walk, moment by moment,
    within my soul's light.*

*

*O Medallion of Preciousness,
may I observe the golden jewels
    of thy diadem,
so that I may know where to
    place the jewel
now close at hand.*

8

THE SPIRITUAL LIFE

Blessed is the man that endureth temptation: for
when he is tried, he shall receive the crown of life,
which the Lord hath promised to them that love him.

—James 1:12

The Third Vitality

All days are eternal days. One should let each day serve the yesterday; and today serve tomorrow in its golden promise of good. He who has energy and not vitality has not the means to use his time.

The spiritual seeker is an eagle by day, surveying the circumference of his action. He is an initiate by night, gaining a godly perspective within the light of his soul. When he learns to blend the energies within his actions, senses, emotions, and thoughts of the day with the vitality of the soul's restoring within the night, he shall receive the *third vitality,* and work within the timeless way of God's intent.

God has made me a namer,
a maker, a creator.
Let me begin now
to name all conditions with praise;
to set aright
past errors with good works;

199

*to create with soul
rather than with self-consciousness.*

*

*May my fearful prudence
become love's expansiveness.
May I know responsiveness.
And may I expand my forgiving
    love.*

*

*Come, voice of my challenger,
and remind me where I am slack;
for I would be done with the
    incessant stumbling,
and begin to put lyrics to the music
of my soul's tone.*

For where two or three are gathered together in
my name, there am I in the midst of them.
—St. Matthew 18:20

United Meditation
When two or three are met in the name of
the Lord Jesus—to blend and mingle their souls'
light—there is a dedicated expectancy to which
the angels respond. From united meditation unusual results occur; lives are transformed.

The spiritual life, when agreed upon by more
than one person, activates a transforming grace.
Into the lives of those who unite their faith
through prayer and meditation will come far
better things in life, in peace, in content. This
contentment is gained gradually; it is not
achieved overnight.

Chaos, clamor, noise, dissension, and con-
fusions intrude upon and prevent the quickening of the soul. Some persons have yet to understand peace. They are insensitive to peace.

Prayers and meditation become a mantle to
insulate one from the unendurable sources of
discord and confusion. Each person has the right
to choose peace or to submit to clamor and dissents. When one consents to dissent and confusion, he hears the harsh musics produced out
of the primitive desires of men. When one
makes the choice of peace, and responds to his
soul, he hears the musics of Heaven.

I rest the pinions of my love
upon my soul's purest light.

*I am immersed in an innermost
     quiet,
where neither force nor fear
can enter in.*

       *

*The very vital strength of my life
     is of God.
I set aside my lesser will
and rest my weakness
upon the Might of God.*

       *

*God is the Source.
I return to Him
as the Source of my being.
I rely upon His Will.
I will obey His Law
spoken through the many tongues
of mediation.*

       *

*My confounders and my confusers
are attracted to me
by my unknowing and unbelieving.
When I know,
my ears will no longer hear
the clamors of dissent.*

And all things, whatsoever ye shall ask in prayer, believing, ye shall receive.
— St. Matthew 21:22

The
Rhythmic
Use of
Prayer

Prayer is a spiritual power. Through the rhythmic use of prayer, the soul—as a mighty bellows for the Spirit—enlarges the range of spiritual experience. Prayer becomes the lightning piercing the dark as a prescient messenger. Impersonal prayers are like wafted strains of music falling into the inner ear of the needy. Continued praying breaks in twain the bonds of binding. Though one often feels unworthy when he prays, he should fear not prayer. The ear of God has many openings. There are many and varied ways in which prayers are answered. God determines how prayers are answered.

My prayers shall go before me,
making ready my heart
to receive the command of love.

Pray without ceasing.

—I Thessalonians 5:17

Selfless Prayer

All prayers are answered. The confirming grace of the soul, accompanying the answer to prayer, works in two manners. When prayer is selfless, the confirming grace of the soul will disclose the miraculous way in which God provides. When prayer is colored by acquisitiveness and self-desire, one is yet unready to coordinate his true needs with his physical wants; the answer to his prayer will be a lesson rather than the receiving of that prayed for. Such a lesson will eventually prepare him to receive the answer to his true needs.

One should come to recognize the answers to his prayers, whether through lessons or actual fulfillment of his desires sent forth in prayer. The more gratitude one feels for all lessons, the greater will be the illumination accompanying prayer.

Selfless prayer is the restrainer of lustful thoughts, the peace-giver to the senses, and the means by which the living substances within the organs of the body are rejuvenated and regenerated.

I will seek to balance my need with the Manifestation of the Father.

*

The words of my prayers
shall become as living pearls,
and build a stair to Heaven.

*

The mediative range of my prayers
is infinite, mighty.
I shall blend my prayers
with the Might and Power of God.

O Lord, how great are thy works! and thy thoughts
are very deep.
—Psalm 92:5

Contemplative Induction   The soul works as a mighty two-way radar,
sending and receiving. Contemplative induction
is the way in which one receives the creative
ideas residing within the soul. Through contemplative induction one learns of the sequential
order of the world; of the Plan of God for
men in the world; of the pattern, the design,
and the way through which one may ethically
fulfill his part of the Plan, pattern, and design.
All persons who have accomplished, achieved,
and attained have used the power of contemplative induction. Through a timely and rhythmic yielding to the soul, one may sustain contemplative induction, and thus become a mighty
channel for the creative ideas sent forth from
the soul.

> *My dimensions are no wider*
> *or broader*
> *than my belief*
> *in the power of my soul.*
>
>   *
>
> *O soul's quiet,*
> *let me know*
> *the Inner Light.*
> *And let all of the audible tongues*
> *in me*
> *speak creatively*
> *for God.*

My soul breaketh for the longing that it hath unto thy judgments at all times. —Psalm 119:20

Soul-
Urgency

In former times, men were more mystically inclined, remaining in prolonged, exalted states of emotional ecstasy. Their exalted states concerned themselves only; they were not concerned with others in the world. The outer pressures of the world today do not permit the spiritual seeker to enter into prolonged periods of ecstatic contemplation. In the present self-genesis age, the spiritual life and the outer life coincide. Spiritual experience accompanies practicality. In the age of self-genesis, all men are under pressure; in the more highly evolved person, this is expressed as a soul-urgency. One should pray to unite the urgency of his soul with the competency demanded of him in his everyday life.

May my hopes become more than wish.
May my desires become living verities,
bringing pure peace, pure love.

Depart from evil, and do good; seek peace, and
pursue it.
                                          —Psalm 34:14

But the fruit of the Spirit is love, joy, peace, long-
suffering, gentleness, goodness, faith.
                                          —Galatians 5:22

Soul-Peace

He who has soul-peace has a grandeur, and
opens the door to greater vistas of love, life,
truth, discovery, joy. Soul-peace comes from a
whole self complemented by many degrees of
divinity. Where there is mediation, there are
degrees of divinity. Where there is meditation,
there is the power to extend the degrees of
mediation.

Love is the yeast through which one expands
his soul-peace. One should pray for discern-
ment, that he might know what is his will and
what is the Will of God. He should say to himself daily, "I trust the Will of God for me."

I seek the serenity
given by the Divine Seraphim.
                    *

I pray for the chiefest virtue—
peace.
                    *

After many trials in mediation,
I shall learn the peace-tongue.
                    *

My whole being yearns
for a sacred and continued peace.
O angel, show me
the pathway to peace.

Continue in prayer, and watch in the same with
thanksgiving; Withal praying also for us, that God
would open unto us a door of utterance, to speak
the mystery of Christ . . .
                                    — Colossians 4:2,3

**The
Believing
Heart**
The believing heart and the unprejudiced
mind are mighty instruments for the illumination power of the soul. When the heart is a
believing heart, the illumination power of the
soul will erase any remaining thoughts of pre-
judging or prejudice. Snap judgments become,
in time, similar to small grains of concrete
which adhere to each thought.

Prejudice plus malice nullifies the soul's
power of illumination. He who is prejudiced
without malice will eventually recognize the
need for spiritual instruction. To open the believing heart and free the thoughts from prejudice, one should pray continually for those who
condemn all things spiritual with thoughtless
and hasty judgments.

One should fortify himself with prayer, that
he may be qualified when called upon to clarify
his beliefs to a prejudiced mind. However, one
is not prepared to instruct the prejudiced mind
until his own thoughts are cleansed of prejudice and judgment.

*I shall agree quickly
to dissolve the prejudiced and
judging thoughts*

set up by the fears
of my lesser will.

*

I pray to overcome the temptation
of a prejudiced mind.
May I behold the glory of the
        uttermost good
in all persons.

For the word of God is quick, and powerful and sharper than any twoedged sword, piercing even to the dividing asunder of soul and spirit, and of the joints and marrow, and is a discerner of the thoughts and intents of the heart.

—Hebrews 4:12

And the world passeth away, and the lust thereof: but he that doeth the will of God abideth for ever.

—I John 2:17

God's Abiding Love

When thought is crystal clear, one is master of his ship. When soul is free, one is master of his fate. The attributes of the soul are God-given. When one is aware of his soul-attributes, he is gifted with a fine mind and a pure heart. When one is sick or weak, his ship is tossed, ridden by winds—and brought under control only through God's abiding love.

God's love provides protection in all distresses and tumults of the body, the heart, and the mind. One is enriched by the unceasing love of God. The soul responds to the love of God. When one draws nigh to his soul and releases to the soul the tumult in his life, God will manifest His abiding love within the soul—and the body will respond. The confusion recorded in the senses will come to rest in the quiet of God's abiding love.

The abiding love of God
gives freedom to my higher will.

*

*My soul will not relinquish its
    purpose;
neither will God desert me.*

*

*He who would stand between me
and the Light of my soul
stands in the shadow
of his own godlessness.*

At that time Jesus answered and said, I thank thee,
O Father, Lord of heaven and earth, because thou
hast hid these things from the wise and prudent,
and hast revealed them unto babes.

—St. Matthew 11:25

The Divining Power of the Soul

When the June rose has had its bloom, and
the mystery between man's blood and soul has
opened its secret; when the autumn leaf has
united its chemistry with the elements of the
earth—then comes the way on which the divining power of the soul reaches, rises, moves, and
turns. Then comes winter. And out of winter
comes the way on which the divining power
of the soul produces wisdom. Winter tempers
man; winter tempers him, that he may turn
again to spring with a renewal of birth and life.

May the divining power of my soul
give enrichment
to my intention.

*

I have earned the divining power
of my soul
through the mastery over the
alternates
and the opposites.

*

My soul waiteth to hear the Lord
speak
with a mighty sound.
May I divine His Word,
and live.

9

ETHICS AND DISCIPLINES

We are as grains of wheat
Waiting to be planted in right
        timing.
And within us
Life pushes forth,
Moving towards the rich earth of
        living.
And we know that when we are
        planted
We shall move upward, freeing
        the life within.
And there shall come the budded
        promise,
The flowers, the seeds.
And we shall be planted again.
God is the Eternal One,
And we are of the Eternal.
In the timeless time of God,
In our eternity,
And in all eternities to come,
We take our Light.

When one dedicates to stand in the Light, and asks to be instructed in the Light, he extends his mental atoms—and thoughts which

have been germinating close to his need come
forth, and disclose creative ideas. Thereafter,
he is quickened in new ways and new works.
One cannot remain the same from day to day.
There is always the Divine order of God's
equation which makes it possible for him to
grow, to progress, and to evolve. When one
seeks a spiritual way, he is quickened in evolvement. *Evolvement* means to have a high purpose
and a high calling beyond the heavier things in
the world.

In the present time, men are burdened because they have believed too much on the im-
mortalizing of material things. Material things
are merely loaned to men; men are but stewards
of possessions and things. When one becomes a
good steward, all things are added unto him.
In the spiritual life, one learns first of the Kingdom of God and of His righteousness. He ob-
serves the ethical laws, that he may become a
good steward, and thus become a righteous
disciple, fulfilling the works of righteousness
through substance and supply.

When one bends himself away from work—
becoming a work-hater, or resisting the various
ways in which he must earn—his supply is cut
off or made short. But when one works with the
rhythm, tide, and rise of labor and creation, this
is evolvement.

Valiant works are works of courage. If one

believes in the spiritual laws, he should live them without fear of the opinions of other men. If he believes in the words and the Ethic of the Lord Jesus, he should live a spiritual life unashamedly. A dedicated person continues quietly, simply, day by day, to live within the framework of a life devoted to God.

A valiant disciple of valiant works dares to manifest the image lying nigh unto his soul. He dares to bring forth new ideas to man— ideas which correlate to God. Ethic must accompany valiant works. Spiritual works come not out of the foolishness of oneself, or out of a spontaneity of ideas which do not correlate to the order of things. But valiant ideas, when correlated to Ethic, produce beauty in creation, and produce a life free of the handicaps which would hem one in and prevent the spiritual life.

Happy is the one who has founded his life upon the eternal laws of God. When one fulfills the laws of God, the Ethic is established; his heart is at peace; his mind is set upon creation beyond worldly attainments. When one creates with pure Ethic, men recognize him as being unique. The intuition of the masses will invariably single out the man of destiny. Only those who have alignment with Ethic may hold the spiritual destinies of other men in their hands, and direct them. When all men come to express the Jesus Ethic, there will be perfect harmony among men, for all shall work with Divine incentive. Their minds and their creativity shall be filled with holy compulsions for the good of all.

Through Ethic one learns to discern the difference between men who *will* for power and men who work within the Will of God. One should pray for holy discrimination. He should revere the selfless works of good. He should seek to avoid being ornate or glamorous; he should dedicate himself to simplicity and purity, that he might become an ethical creator within the Will of God.

One who moves beyond decaying standards into spiritual Ethic maintains his poise in time of peril. His extended perception will enable him to present a loving reassurance to those with fearful hearts. He inspires others to love God and to cherish His good.

Dedication is a responsibility. Dedication is also the surrender of the lesser will to the Will of God. When one dedicates, he should be prepared to undergo cataclysmic changes. These changes begin first in the inner world. The last and final cataclysm comes from without. Having proven himself to the inner self, one must also prove himself to the outer world, and particularly to those who are associated with him in the personal and intimate relationships. Very often, those near by who love him with mortal love resent the transition in temperament, in motive, and in design. Should this occur in the life of the one who dedicates, he should pray that in all relationships he may be more kind, more flexible, more tender. The strength he has gained through his dedication will sustain him in many and varied ways.

All persons entering the spiritual life are in some degree dedicated. However, until one is free to totally dedicate himself, he will suffer some oppositions and intrusions as to his beliefs and way of life. These should be patiently borne by the disciple until such time as his soul and his grace will see fit to free him for a totally dedicated life. The confirmation of a total dedication comes when others in the world recognize the spiritual purpose in the life of the dedicated disciple. In this recognition is also a reverent observing of the right to choice and privacy as essential to the spiritual life. When the disciple experiences this confirming, more shall be required of him; for others in the world will come to lean, consciously, upon his spiritual strength. If the disciple has failed to receive the confirmation of his dedication, he should continue to observe the Ethic. In time he will find that the angels will confirm his dedication through certain helps. There is no greater joy than working under the mantle of angelic approval.

The story of Jacob and the ladder is a story of communing with the Angelic World and the finer degrees of Light in Heaven. Man is a soul with a mind. His feelings and his thoughts may be comely and Divine instruments for creation. Step by step, each person must climb the ladder, or be lifted up into intercommunion with God. To do so, he must deny himself, and live in the world under the staff of discipline, justice, mercy.

A spiritual life is more than belief. A spiritual life consists of an unwavering faith, a stewardship of properties, an ethical responsibility toward one's fellow men. Men are not yet perfect; but all are given the opportunity to try. When one is true in his actions or works, the diadem of his soul's light will instruct him. His mind will be illumined; and he will turn his face toward the Light of the Christ.

Therefore all things whatsoever ye would that men
should do to you, do ye even so to them.
— St. Matthew 7:12

I. THE ETHIC OF CONSIDERATION

Respect the potential and innate chastity of
each person, and look for his purity rather than
his moral errors.

*To discipline away vulgar or irreverent thoughts
pertaining to sex, make more chaste your attitude toward procreation. Make immaculate
your thoughts about birth. Be thankful for the
unending thread of generation which makes
all men one.*

*

Avoid manipulating the will of another. This
includes father, mother, brother, sister, husband,
wife, child, friend, acquaintance.

*To discipline an unruly will, obey the voice of
your conscience, and thus become free of the
manipulative wills of other persons.*

*

Permit each person to discover and, therefore,
to experience. Thus, you will bring the timing
of your own creation into order.

*To discipline the tendency to act out of timing,
refuse to yield to the sensuous side of your
senses. Let your senses become pure perceivers.
Let your imagination be a vehicle for true
imaging.*

*

Be wholly loving.

To discipline unruly desires, search your love motive, and cleanse away possessiveness, jealousy, hatred, prejudice. Give your love sincerely, fully, completely.

*

Refuse to despoil the character of anyone with gossip.

To discipline the tongue, the instrument of logos, make a covenant to speak only words of truth. Refrain from careless conversation, and keep alive the vowel of love within speech and word. Have periods each day of silent serenity. Unite your heart's love with your intelligence. Let your speech be truthful, peaceful, rational.

*

Think of the success of others with joy. Be grateful that others have earned their beautiful possessions, their talents, their loving friends.

To discipline an imprudent imagination, refrain from condemnation, judgment. Envision the soul-grace and pure prototypal presence of each person; and look for the angel standing nigh each one.

*

Consider your body, your emotions and your thoughts as potential skills for God's creation. Make holy your personality and its works. Learn to be a mighty overcomer.

To discipline the physical, etheric, emotional, and mental bodies, let the cosmos in you unite with the cosmic, the spirit with the soul, the soul with the mind, the mind with the heart, and the heart with the living image of the body. Sustain this vision—and remember, the eternal in you works for perfection.

Who shall ascend into the hill of the Lord? or who shall stand in his holy place? He that hath clean hands, and a pure heart; who hath not lifted up his soul unto vanity, nor sworn deceitfully. He shall receive the blessing from the Lord, and righteousness from the God of his salvation.

—Psalm 24:3-5

But seek ye first the kingdom of God, and his
righteousness; and all these things shall be added
unto you.
                                    —St. Matthew 6:33

II. THE ETHIC PERTAINING TO
MATERIAL POSSESSIONS

Be responsible, dependable, and reliable. Determine to become a good steward of your own possessions and a scrupulous steward when entrusted with the possessions of others.

To discipline wanton waste and disregard for possessions of self or others, determine to spend prudently, frugally, carefully.

*

Overcome envy and covetousness. Rejoice in the prosperity of others.

To discipline yourself as to greed, avarice, covetousness, give lovingly to others what you would desire for yourself.

*

Be willing at all times to share your material possessions—and, in some instances, to relinquish them.

To discipline traits of cupidity and acquisitiveness, and to avoid covetousness and jealousy from others as to your possessions, be unostentatious; refrain from smugness; never feel exceptionally blessed as to your possessions.

*

Fulfill with honor your material and financial obligations.

To discipline the tendency to desire things, devoid of effort, recognize material possessions to be the result of effort, past or present. Generate a continued gratitude to our Father, the Manifestor of all things and persons in the world.

*

Conduct yourself with integrity as to authority or command over material possessions.

To discipline the inclination to misuse your grace, give without thought of return; act without thought of reward.

*

Never permit your blind indulgences or shortsighted charities to interfere with a person's capacity and opportunity to earn. Let your charities be for those who are the hapless victims of the evils in the world.

To discipline negative thought images, which result in poverty, disappointment and hardship, think on the Substance of God as bountifully yours in right timing; work for the love of work rather than for recognition.

*

Become a good craftsman with whatever material has been given to you as a workman for God. Revere the works of your hands; and create without thought of earning. Let the glory of God and His righteousness increase your possessions and make bountiful your provision.

To discipline yourself when doubting manifestation, do all things through the Will of God; listen constantly for guidance; and read frequently the Parable of the Fishes and the Loaves as manifested through the Lord Jesus.

And he commanded the multitude to sit down on the grass, and took the five loaves, and the two fishes, and looking up to heaven, he blessed and brake, and gave the loaves to his disciples, and the disciples to the multitude.

—St. Matthew 14:19

**He that loveth father or mother more than me is
not worthy of me; and he that loveth son or
daughter more than me is not worthy of me.**

—St. Matthew 10:37

III. THE ETHIC FOR FAMILY RELATIONSHIPS

Lovingly fulfill all duties towards persons
related by blood, remembering that the soul of
each one did choose the ties of blood and family.

*Refrain from resentment when the burdens of
the family fall upon you and you alone. Give
praise that the compass of your soul knows your
strength, your skill, your need.*

*

Remain an individual; and give each member of the family the right to have individual
expression, thought, and action.

*Overcome any tendency to deflation or infla-
tion when a member of the family is made
prominent by blame or praise. Remember,
when one makes reverent his association with
those of blood, his soul will then extend his ties
to the Family of the World.*

*

Even as a bride and bridegroom must forsake
their parents for one another, so also should one
cease to depend upon his blood relationships to
materially support or morally sustain him once
he has entered into a spiritual life.

Should you be separated from the family ties through placement, marriage, distance, or estrangement, resolve to adjust this relationship through releasing love.

*

Determine to think charitably of ancestry, yet avoid dwelling overmuch upon family pride and achievement.

Overcome the tendency to tribal-genesis pride through selfless achievement which will exemplify your past, present, and future.

*

Relinquish any thought of material inheritance from relatives or blood-tie persons.

Think charitably as to unpaid loans, diverted inheritances, or seeming injustices rendered by conniving blood relatives. Relinquish any resentment as to parental preferences for sisters and brothers.

*

Think always of your Father in Heaven as your true Father. Turn to Him for moral and spiritual support.

Overcome a claiming dependency or tendency to lean upon the family assets. Enlarge the horizon of your family-atom by reflecting upon the grace uniting and fortifying the ties of blood.

*

Know that all persons of the earth are your brothers and sisters in the Christ.

Each day accept the strength sent forth from the grace of the soul. Rise above dissents made possible through the intimacy of kinship. Remember, even the Holy Family-Atom contained persons with varied degrees of evolvement.

For whosoever shall do the will of my Father which is in heaven, the same is my brother, and sister, and mother.   —St. Matthew 12:50

Now ye are clean through the word which I have spoken unto you.
                                        —St. John 15:3

IV. THE ETHIC OF PURITY

Remove all prudish, lustful, sensuous, and irreverent attitudes toward the procreative act. *Discipline your sentient palate through a taste for only pure and unpolluted foods.*

*

Search your dominant emotions. Analyze your desires. Resolve to cleanse away forcefulness, or undue pressure upon any one or any thing. *Utilize your time with orderly, active industry. Give heed to justice, and waste not your life's substance through anger and resentment.*

*

Learn from Nature the secret of the cleansing fire within the air you breathe, the water you drink, the food you eat, the earth you walk upon. *Sustain a permanent state of thankfulness and gratitude toward God. Acknowledge Him as your provision. Look not toward man's destruction. Determine to become a channel for the bounteous life-substance of God working in you, through you, and of you.*

*

Love purely all persons. *Let your love be close to the theme of selfless giving. Be generous with your adjectives of love, praise, admiration, cheer. Remember, all whom you love are a projection of yourself.*

*

Speak truthfully of each person. Let your words injure no man.

Dignify your own person by becoming reliable as to what you say, what you promise, what you do.

*

Contemplate the pure, the true, the good.

To feel free to say, "I am of God," accept the reprovings from your conscience; and obey the guidance of your conscience within three days— by trying to set aright the pattern of disorder weighing so heavily upon your emotions and thoughts.

*

The reward for purity on all levels will be "Blessed are the pure in heart: for they shall see God."

Build a step a day to your Higher Self by contemplating the many ways offered to you to purify your actions, emotions, and thoughts.

Let no man despise thy youth; but be thou an example of the believers, in word, in conversation, in charity, in spirit, in faith, in purity.

—I Timothy 4:12

And whosoever shall exalt himself shall be abased;
and he that shall humble himself shall be exalted.
—St. Matthew 23:12

V. THE ETHIC OF AUTHORITY

Refrain from making decisions *for* any mature person. Show the two ways: the left and the right—and their consequences. And let the person decide for himself.

Agree with your soul to accept full responsibility for your actions, emotions, and thoughts.

*

In authority over animals, children, the helpless, and the immature, be obedient to the Good Law of God; and pray for guidance, wisdom, and charity, so as to instruct and guide rather than decide.

Refuse to yield to angry, aggressive, belligerent thoughts, words, deeds.

*

Never accept an assignment for the sake of authority.

Learn to use incentive, and to free your initiative by carrying your full part of the load.

*

If your grace has placed you in a position of authority, strive each day to learn self-mastery and humility.

Give thanks to the Father for accomplishment. Be careful to avoid self-praise.

*

At all times, avoid dominating attitudes. One may stand in the Will of God when he ceases being the will for others.

Each one has a special talent, qualifying him to excel someone else. Do not fail to remember that others also possess and express some special thing for God.

*

Assume responsibility with respect for the expectations of others.

Remember, you are the guardian of the trust others place in you. Try to justify this trust by going a second "mile" with that one who places his trust in you.

*

Pray to be found worthy in the sight of the Lord. Learn to live with and be faithful to the Good Law of God. Remember the words of Jesus: "And whosoever of you will be the chiefest, shall be servant of all. For even the Son of man came not to be ministered unto, but to minister, and to give his life a ransom for many."

Each day, upon arising, make a dedication and a covenant—that God's Will shall guide you. When you say, "God's Will be done," do not forget that your words are heard in Heaven. Accept His Will and abide therein.

And whosoever shall compel thee to go a mile, go with him twain.
                                        —St. Matthew 5:41

**Heal the sick, cleanse the lepers, raise the dead,
cast out devils: freely ye have received, freely give.**

— St. Matthew 10:8

VI. THE ETHIC OF HEALING

Dedicate your healing-ministry works to God.

First observe the rules of your own body, that you may more ethically concern yourself with the well-being of others.

*

Develop the impersonal sympathy, and sustain compassion toward all suffering.

Hold no aversion for the deformed, the retarded, the crippled.

*

Before beginning your healing prayers and healing procedure, purify yourself; activate the etheric sanitation by cleansing the body, emotions, and thoughts.

At some time each day, search inwardly, so as to discern the action of your four bodies: the physical, the emotional, the etheric, the mental.

*

"Judge not, that ye be not judged." Remain unprejudiced as to the debt concealed within the suffering of the one to be helped.

Observe the silent logos. Refrain from discussing any person who looks to you for spiritual, mediative helps.

*

Cauterize the illness by holding the person in the Light. (Use the Niscience technique of holding in the Light.) In mantramic speaking, do not speak directly to the person to be healed; speak only to the Angel of the person, with mantramic words of love.

Never feel that your healing prayers are wasted. Give freely within the Healing Technique and Ethic of the Niscience practices. Limit not God by limiting your desire to serve.

*

In the recovering phase of sickness, if the Niscience instruction is requested, give the Niscience instruction with impartiality, gentleness and love. If the Niscience instruction is properly given, the conscience of the person suffering and the illumination faculty of his soul will interpret and reveal to him the hidden cause within the sickness. The Niscience Healing Minister should patiently await the flowering forth of the revealing aspect in the sickness, and should not personally disclose to the one sick the root-cause of his sickness, or else the Healing Minister will assume some of the karmic burden of the one sick.

Remove all aggressiveness in your will. Come to peace within yourself. Avoid negative encounters with the will of the one you would help to heal.

*

Each day pray that the Father will lead you to those who have need of healing helps and Niscience instruction. Most important: Think not of yourself as being the healer. Be continually aware of and thankful for the heavenly, healing helps of Mediation.

Revitalize your faith each day. Remain true to your mediative rhythms, so as to become a fluidic, healing instrument for God. Remember: he who fails to discipline himself will be impoverished for self, and impotent for God.

And he stood over her, and rebuked the fever; and it left her: and immediately she arose and ministered unto them.   —St. Luke 4:39

In your patience possess ye your souls.

—St. Luke 21:19

VII. THE ETHIC OF ASSOCIATION

One should accept his placement as to family. He should not feel superior or inferior to his relatives.

Pray to unravel and understand the karmic family-threads in association. Do not live for any person, *be he relative or friend. Let all relationships come to terms with Light, and each association will become a manifestation of selfless love.*

*

In contemplating marriage, one should be yoked with a believer. (II Corinthians 6:14) Husband and wife should look to God as the Authority in their marriage, rather than to outer circumstance or persons.

If marriage is the product of the vibratory hum of the soul's medallion, know that you agreed to the disciplines within partnership. If marriage be ended by divorcement due to a situation out of your control, accept the lesson; be charitable toward the past, and flexible toward the promise within God's Plan for you.

*

In business, one should be a craftsman in his work and honorable in his business placement.

At all times, he should seek to use creative initiative in his work; but he should also remember that, "Whosoever will be chief among you, let him be your servant."

Be not the aggressor nor the despot in work environment. Learn to appreciate the creative powers of those who work with you. Remember: if the Angels worked with dissensions, man would live in continual darkness.

*

In one's social obligations and friendships, he should remember that lasting friendships are sustained through constancy, loyalty, sacrifice.

Respect your friends and revere friendship. Keep the confidence of a friend, and you will be rewarded with the powers obtained from silent logos.

*

One should fill his heart and mind with love when he thinks upon and contemplates the humanities, remembering that all men are children of the Father, and are also the potential sons of God.

Search out race prejudice within yourself; cleanse it; refuse to let it enter into your heart, your thoughts. Wherever race injustice is present, speak for the humanities and God's Plan for His children in the world. Pray for at least ten people each day; increase the number when

*you feel so inclined. Do not forget the ten lepers;
one did remember.*

*

Race. Race and racial placement fulfill the
Will of God. One should revere his placement
in race and the placement of others in their
races; and he should remember at all times that
there is an invisible law governing all races.
Nation. One should understand that nations live
and die, even as men live and die; that nations
may reach heights in their destinies; and that
nations may err, even as men—but one should
look to the Archetype of a nation and see its
intent for the many in national placement.

*Remember, there are patriots and statesmen.
There are also bigots in politics, as there are
bigots in religion. Determine to pray for justice
within your nation, and honor for your country.
Recognize that nations err as men err. Speak
to the Angels of the Archetype of the nation.
Pray that peace and love will return to men.*

*

In the spiritual life, one should remember
that he is a yoke fellow correlated to his fellow
disciple, working continually in Mediation. In
some instances, he may be co-atom to a fellow
disciple. One should avoid exploiting his fellow
disciple. He must refrain from seeking to benefit, materially or socially, from a fellow disciple.

One should be willing to sacrifice for his fellow disciple, to forgive his fellow disciple, and to aid his fellow disciple. However, in certain initiatory trials, one should refrain from intruding upon the experience of his fellow disciple. In such extreme conditions, his knowledge of the Ethic and his work with the Angels will enable him to selflessly and silently *stand by* and serve.

Overcome any feeling of repulsion for any associate student in the spiritual life, even though he be a Judas disciple. Pray for him that his Angel come unto him to lift him.

And forgive us our debts, as we forgive our debtors.
—St. Matthew 6:12

But God said unto him, Thou fool, this night thy soul shall be required of thee: then whose shall those things be, which thou hast provided?

—St. Luke 12:20

VIII. THE ETHIC OF INHERITANCE

Covet not the possessions of others; and become a good steward of your grace, your material possessions, your talents, your friendships, your responsibilities and authorities.

Each day devote a few moments to self-research. Let your True Self ask the little will what stewardship has meant each day. Determine to master the following responsibilities: joyfully earn your livelihood; be hospitable with sincerity; be generous with complete detachment; return to the storehouse of the Father the first fruits of your labors.

*

Be free of egotism and affectation. Expand and make nobler, in this life, the talents you have inherited from former lives.

Look inward, and evaluate how versatile you are. Do you emphasize one quality more than another? Seek to give balance to your especial uniqueness, so as to obtain a harmonious contentment gained from perfect expression.

*

Envy is the greatest foe of love; therefore, envy not any man, his talents, his material possessions, his friendships, his acclaim or rewards. *Do not permit the acidity of criticism to enter into your thoughts as related to the progress of others. Rejoice in the good news for others, even though it may mean sacrifice for you.*

*

Avoid the presumption that any one is lucky or fortunate; for each thing possessed has been earned wholly by the possessor.

Give praise to God for His Equation. Dwell often upon the words, "The Father 'sendeth rain on the just and on the unjust'."

*

Refrain from identifying any person with the faults of his ancestors; and look not for inherited, negative ancestral resemblances and traits in your child, husband, wife, brother, sister, friend.

Learn to look with joy upon the Cosmic Whole. Think often upon the reincarnation tidal waves; the many and varied approaches needed in the world for experiences and expression. Give every man the chance to become himself.

*

Revere the great examples of nobility left by men no longer living. Forgive the faults of the dead, so as to aid the dead to rise. And give thanks that the Guardian Angel and Recording Angel watch over him who sleepeth, and that the greater Judge, the Christ, is the Judge of both dead and living. Refrain from earth-binding the dead by misuse of inheritance from the dead, or by being embittered that one did not inherit from the dead. And covet not the possessions of one close to the state of death.

In receiving telepathy from the dead during sleep, or during waking hours, bless them in the name of the Christ—and leave them in the Light.

*

At all times, remember that the only true inheritance you possess is Eternal Life. Relate each thing in life to this attitude, and you shall possess deathless possessions . . . "a treasure in the heavens that faileth not, where no thief approacheth, neither moth corrupteth. For where your treasure is, there will your heart be also." (St. Luke 12:33,34)

Forget not the words: "Bless them that curse you, do good to them that hate you." Remember, if the Father did not so will it, no one could take from you your honor, your health, your possessions, your loved ones. Question yourself if you are lacking in any of these. Give thanks that "your Father knoweth what things ye have need of, before ye ask him."

. . . thy rod and thy staff they comfort me.
—Psalm 23:4

Thou shalt love the Lord thy God with all thy heart,
and with all thy soul, and with all thy mind.
—St. Matthew 22:37

IX. THE ETHIC OF WORSHIP

Place no stumbling block in the way of anyone regarding his technique and procedure in worship. Recognize the need in each one to seek God; and respect the procedures in all worships.

Determine to ignore the unthinking words or scathing statements of others pertaining to your source of worship. Remember, Jesus is the Door to all true teachings of the Father.

*

Examine the religious intent within your heart and mind. Ask yourself, "Do I worship religion, or God?"

Look not for fine places of worship. Learn to recognize that a building devoid of true liberty can become confinement or a prison to those who worship form.

*

Determine that your worship of God means first the love of God, of His creation, and of all His creatures.

Worship not any man or person. Only God, the Incomprehensible, is that One to whom we may turn with awe.

*

Pray to find a worship which contains the answers to the need in your heart, mind, and soul. Remain loyal, constant and faithful to the source of your instruction, which directs your way of worship and longing for God.

Listen to the inherent intuition of your soul. Avoid enticements and meandering tongues.

*

Be joyful, and rejoice that you may contribute and tithe to your spiritual home of worship. Lovingly serve and helpfully support your spiritual home of worship, thus preserving your way of worship. In this, you will make it possible for others in the world to share your way of worship.

A worship which fails the flesh, the soul, and the Spirit is anathema to God's intent for you.

*

Be not obstinate in your religious beliefs, but be firm and assured in your faith in God. Enter not into controversy with others as to your worship. Look deep within your heart each day, and dissolve any remaining prejudice, dogma, bigotry, and persecution.

Your faith correlates to one of the prisms of Light emanating from God. Try each day to see each man's feeble interpretation of God as a trial towards a greater degree of faith within the Light.

*

Turn with complete trust to the *vortice pool* of your worship. Know it to be but the outer temple for the inner and holy temple of God. Absorb all it seeks to give you. Be reverent and diligent in your studies, so that you may better serve God, and therefore worship Him "in spirit and in truth."

Trust your soul to guide you, and your intuition to lead you to your spiritual home. With uttermost joy, be glad for your spiritual home.

Heaven and earth shall pass away, but my words shall not pass away.   — St. Matthew 24:35

And whosoever doth not bear his cross, and come
after me, cannot be my disciple.

—St. Luke 14:27

X. THE ETHIC OF SPIRITUAL EXALTATION

One should begin by counting the cost of a
spiritual life; that is, he should understand that
a spiritual life is a life of sacrifice and selfless
service.

*Be not disturbed when others criticise you for
your way of life. Be patient with unthinking
persons. Remain impenetrable to those who
ridicule your faith.*

*

Move with the tide of your evolvement.
Glorify God and gratefully accept the initiations of today and the coming initiations of
tomorrow.

*When things appear more difficult, make a
covenant to increase your prayers.*

*

Remember that only the strong are *chosen.*
Look to Mediation for help and succor in time
of need.

*Once the decision to live the spiritual life has
been made, look not back.*

*

Be wary, lest you fall into the pitfall of spiritual pride. Resolve to be faithful, competent,
and daring for Christ's sake.

Keep each promise to yourself as though it were a covenant with God.

*

Understand thoroughly your responsibility as a disciple. Be charitable toward those who are yet to understand.

Resolve to speak your faith through the commonplace—that is, let the Word of God use your voice each day.

*

Be unyieldingly positive where antichrist is present.

Do not enter into controversy with fanatics, but never let Satan win an argument.

*

Persecute no man, remembering "Vengeance is mine; I will repay, saith the Lord."

Avoid being a karmic policeman. Remember the words of Jesus: "Agree with thine adversary quickly, whiles thou art in the way with him; lest at any time the adversary deliver thee to the officer, and thou be cast into prison." St. Matthew 5:25.

And Jesus said unto him, No man, having put his hand to the plow, and looking back, is fit for the kingdom of God.
—St. Luke 9:62

Give not that which is holy unto the dogs, neither
cast ye your pearls before swine, lest they trample
them under their feet, and turn again and rend you.

—St. Matthew 7:6

XI. THE ETHIC FOR THE USE OF THE DEEPER SPIRITUAL MYSTERIES

Make yourself trustworthy, so that you will
attract an honorable company of listeners and
doers.

*Rule out antagonism, curiosity, and prejudice
toward the religions of others.*

*

Be prepared to speak of your faith with simplicity. Learn to know and define what you
believe of God, for he who has not a name for
his praise lives in a shadowed world.

*Think of the Angelic Guardians protecting the
worships of men.*

*

Be not hasty to convert everyone; remember
your past uncertainties. And, forget not—the
joy of discovery is a gift from God.

*Fill your mind with gratitude for the True
Sacraments of Heaven, which overdwell the
worships of men.*

*

When someone continues to lean on your spiritual strength, he is ripe for the higher instruc-

tion. Learn to recognize one who looks to you to point the way. Become a responsible mediator—and give sole credit to the higher powers of Mediation.

Respect the sincerity in the priesthood and ministry in all religions. Overcome the tendency to look for human fault in the ministry or priesthood.

*

Do not jump to the conclusion that you possess all the answers. Always remember there is one true Saviour, and that there are many steps to be climbed to reach Him.

When there are dry spells, give thanks for the time of reflection. Prepare for the challenger after the quiet time.

*

Be alert each moment as to the part you play in speaking the Word of God. Be what you believe, and activate your spiritual knowledge—and your *own* will hear the Word within your voice.

Give thanks that one cannot serve two masters; for compromise would rend you in twain.

*

To avoid persecution in wrong timing, "Be ye therefore wise as serpents, and harmless as doves." Be not fretful, for tensions attract attention from the darkened wills of men. Trust in the discrimination of the Higher Worlds, "for many are called, but few are chosen."

Each day learn of contentment. Overcome the resistance to discipline.

Let a man so account of us, as of the ministers of Christ, and stewards of the mysteries of God.
—I Corinthians 4:1

For all the prophets and the law prophesied until
John. And if ye will receive it, this is Elias, which
was for to come. He that hath ears to hear, let
him hear.
                                    —St. Matthew 11:13-15

XII. THE ETHIC OF REVELATION

Make orderly your inner and outer circumference. Hold fast to the truth that all men experience repeated lives.

Obey the prompting of your conscience.

*

Do not jump to intellectual conclusions as to the identity of the past life of anyone; wait to have the past-life identity confirmed by the Higher Worlds. To become free of the judgment of men, judge no man. Manipulate no man. Be not retaliative. Inflict no wrong upon the honor or body of any man.

Respond to the guidance of your soul.

*

Avoid irreverent remarks and discussions as to past lives. Relate yourself to the Inner Self in each one, seeing the personality as a composite of many selves.

Cultivate a sweetness, softness, and tenderness in your word-approach to those who are unknowing.

*

Be prepared to explain and to expand the reality of one's having lived in former times or periods. Love the soul of each one. Respect the creative potential in each one. See the hope of the restorative life in all persons.

Offend not the logos through controversy. Develop the wait-and-see power. Trust to the Presences for the mighty result of silence in right timing.

*

Expect to receive your records of past lives from time to time. Be aware of the danger in your present life of placing too much emphasis upon the achievements of past lives. Be not absorbed in the credits gained from past lives. Think not of yourself as exceptional to men, but as one *with* them. Think of yourself as of oneness *in* God. Ennoble God's plan for you by being more worthy each day, and by fulfilling the words: "Therefore all things whatsoever ye would that men should do to you, do ye even so to them."

Jesus said, "Why callest thou me good? none is good, save one, that is, God." Be aware at all times of the soul's record, revealing the errors and the grace. Be a balancer of your grace through charity toward all men. Overcome critical thinking and analytical thought by using the discriminating insight.

*

Overcome your debts of past lives by service and ministering unto men. Remember, the Lord Jesus and His mediators help you to bear the burden of past lives and the burdens of this life. Be reposed within the angelic ministrations. Be filled with the charity of good intent. Be magnified with the healing, ministering Presences.

Be a willing yoke fellow. Remember, a masterbuilder builds for the Eternals.

*

Work with your Recording Angel each day at dusk to restore the memory of God's Eternal Will, Eternal Life, Eternal Light, and Eternal Love for you. Report to your soul as to the use of the hours and moments of your day just past. Be prepared to accept the incoming tide of your reflections and contemplation. Move with the upward ascent. Become responsible, and joyfully accept the Eternal Justice and Equation of God.

Develop your demanifestation and manifestation powers at dusk each day. Work with the justice attribute of your soul. Face and determine to overcome your impulsive thoughts and selfish acts of the past day. Acknowledge your errors, and agree to rectification in the coming days. Remember: Hierarchy, with the Recording Angels, on the last day of this Eter-

nity will retrospect the actions of all men, so as to develop the "face of the waters" for the next Eternity Day.

> **For the Son of man shall come in the glory of his Father with his angels; and then he shall reward every man according to his works.**
>
> **—St. Matthew 16:27**

THE END

INDEX

A

angel(s) 17,31,72,81,87,90,96,101,104,118,124,142,179-181,
     191, 194,201,208,218,219,221,234,237-239,248,253
        Benign 60
        Guardian 50,68,109,110,113,119,121,140,175,188,
           231,241,248
        of Hope 104
        Judgment 50
        Ministering 100
        Recording 49,50,109,113,188,241,253
        Righteousness 143,188
animals 231
archetypes 18,41,43,46,51,67,98,238
art 48
atom(s) 41,64,165
        co- 238
        emotional 41
        eternal 7,45
        eternal sustaining 166
        family 227,228
        heart 29,197
        higher etheric 155
        indestructible 45
        luminosity 155,156,162
        mental 41,214
        physical 41
        sacred 121,160
        sentient 32,161
        spiritual 3,7,46

B

beauty 124,127,137,189,216,221
body, emotional 3,21,22,32,41,111,222,233
        etheric 111,222,233
        everlasting 13,46
        mental 3,111,222,233
        physical 3,14,18,61,111,124,151,165,222,233
brain 43,151

C

character 128,221
charity 72,135,148,174,175,224,231,252,253
Christ 12,103,107,119,161,176,181,219,228,242,246
    Jesus 19
    Light 51,84
    Mind 45,50,178,187
Commandments of God 133
conscience 7,8,23,27,32,33,40,109-122,124,130,161,220,230,
    234,251
consciousness 41,79
consideration 2,220
contemplation 8,9,25,26,34-37,39-41,45,46,65,91,155,170,
    190,206,207,237
Cornucopia of Substance 81,82
crisis 69,70,115

D

death 13,27,46,151,158,242
dedication 3,11,20,25,29,48,75,91,111,126,127,133,136,159,
    170,214,217,218,232,233
devotion 30,75
Diamond Medallion 49
discipleship 25,45,151,163
discipline(s) 29,107,170,183,219-254
Divine Spirit 176,177
dreams 9,27

E

ego 26,37
egotistical shell 111,112,163,172,173
Elect 157
emanation 7,12
emotional body 3,21,22,32,41,111,233
Equation of God 61-63,77,103,113,143,178,215,241,253
esoteric 24,40
eternal life 242,253
    self 40
    spirit 12,46
    sustaining atom 166
etheric body 111,233
    lesser 144
ethic of
    association 236-239
    authority 231,232

consideration 220-222
deeper spiritual mysteries, use of 248-250
family relationships 226-228
healing 233-235
inheritance 240-242
material possessions 223-225
purity 229,230
revelation 251-254
spiritual exaltation 246,247
worship 243-245
ethic(s) 18,28,48,62,63,67,71,72,84,111,117,121,128,132,
185,186,215-254
everlasting body 13,46
life 49
self 153
evolvement 20,41,57,69,70,89,116,119,158,168,215,228,246

F

faith 6,12,34,57,59,62,76,86,93,117,132,157,160,183,235,
244,246-248
family 226-228,236
atom 227,228
fasting 18
Father 12,27,28,30-33,77,93,130,142,159,191,204,224,227,
231,235,237,240,241,243
Fiat, Life 42
Light 42
Love 115,116
food 229
forgiving 23,76,77,137,159,163,173,175,200,241
former lives 3,5-7,34-36,48,49,69,73,79,126,144,158,240,252
friends 221,236,237
friendship 61,237,240,241

G

genius 35,69,111,123
good guile 105,106
Good Law 103,107,231,232
grace
benign 59
chastity 79
consummation 150
creative 48
day-by-day 48,86

divine 51
eternal 49,50,71,113
felicity 77
healing 50
posterity 75
protection 73
provident 81-84
sacred, or sacrifice 49
sanctification 86,87
soul- 26,27,57,58,61,62,65,68,165,197,204
soul-grace & timing 67
tones 91
transforming 48
treasures of 65
world 50
gravity 7,15,22,50,69,92,153
Guardian Angel 50,68,109,110,113,119,121,140,175,188,
    231,241,248
guidance 27,31,41,105,225,230,251

H

healer 3,14,28,62,120,134,138,235
healing 12,14,17,18,25,36,48,51,60,62,77,94,99,101,140,
    144,146,148,152,158-160,163,167,182,198,233-235
Heavenly Host 25
Heavenly Presences 17,31
hierarchy 22,175,253
higher etheric body 46
higher self 26,28,35,36,40-44,49,75,79,80,155-157,161,166,
    198,230
Higher World 17,75,186,250,251
Holy Ghost 18
Holy Presences 17,31,77,252,253
Holy Spirit 129
hope 106,140,157,162,194,207,252

I

ideas 25,35,40,45,123,178,179,206,215,216
Illuminati 50
illumination 7,12,95,119,156,204,209,219,234
individuality 26,34-36,57,186,196
initiation 116,151,163,239,246
inspiration 12,58,123,175
imagination 10,220,221
immortality 75,124

J

Jacob 219
Jesus 28-30,32,33,50,66,67,77,167,190,196,198,201,216,225,
232,243,247,253
    Ethic 216
justice 18,28,61,121,122,178,188,197,219,238,253

K

karma 111,160,162,234,236,247
Kingdom of Heaven 186
    of God 215

L

Law(s) of God 4,7,18,67,70,103,121,122,190,194,197,216
liberty 168,243
Life Fiat 42,159
Life Spirit 79
Light of Christ 12
    of God 12,165,253
Light Fiat 42
Light, magnet of 59
    World of 179
lives, former 3,5-7,34-36,48,49,69,73,79,126,144,158,240,252
    past 37,156,159,251-253
    previous 2,48
logos 41,91,138,159,163,166,221,233,237,252
Lord of Love 163
Lord's Prayer 29,30
Love Fiat 115,116
Love of God 6,11,14,29,78,134,165,197,211,253
luminosity atoms 155,156,162

M

magic 103,194
mantram(s) 8,9,42,44,91,98,99,234
marriage 227,236
martyrdom 49
medallion of the soul 1-3,7-12,33,65,79,117,119,121,197,236
mediation 28,35,40,57,66,100,176,178,187,189,202,208,233,
235,238,246,249,253
meditation 8,9,24-26,35-37,39-46,53,64,155,170,201,208
Melchizedek 51
mental body 3,41,111,222,233
mercy 2,18,28,59,62,87,93,121,191,193,219
metaphysical 24

miracle 103,160,204
money 11,61
music(s) 48,86,165,200,201

N

nation(s) 113,238
Nature 18,68,229
Niscience 178,234,235

O

occult 24,39

P

past lives 37,156,159,251-253
patience 101,181
personality 26,27,34,36,57,58,128,193,221,251
physical body 3,14,18,41,61,111,124,151,165,222,233
physical world 15,26,63,132
pineal gland 12
pituitary gland 11
Plan of God 13,18,22,59,133,206,236,237
Power of God 27,39,194,205
praise 30,100,118,157,199,230
Presence of God 100,252,253
previous lives 2,48
procreation 220,229
pro-genesis 121
prophets 16,113
psychic 19,39,41-43
pulsation 7,12,13,46
purity 93,113,229,230

Q

quiescence 176
quiet 91,176,189,202,206,249

R

race(s) 28,237,238
radiation 7,11
Realm of Light 50
Recording Angel(s) 49,50,109,113,188,241,253
reincarnation 241,251
religion(s) 39,113,238,243,244,248,249
reverence 2,11,19,30,32,45,57,108,116,123,133,145,158,161,
    162,197,226,245
Rhythm of God 4,5,13,123,124,132
ritual 156

S

sacrifice 5,11,65,79,86,131,144,152,161,163,237,239,241,246
sages 16,89
saint(s) 53,86,87,113,130,163,186,196
Saviours 16,50,249
Second Heaven 50
Self, Eternal 40
    -genesis 207
    Inner 251
    Perfect 189
    True 240
sense(s) 9,13-21,32,43,109,110,123,126,142,146,147,176,199,
    204,220
   sixth 17
Seraphim 208
sex 220
sleep 241,242
soul
  attributes 211
  conscience and 109-122
  counsel of 89
  crisis and 69
  divining power of 213
  dynamic power of 186
  and the ethic 132
  faculties 13-15,17-20,22,32,115,123,126,192
  germinal quality within 157
  gifts of 71
  golden veil of 53
  good guile and 105
  grace and timing 67
  healing power of 146
  jewel of 55,63
  -life 36
  -love 36,136
  mantrams and 99
  medallion of 1,3,7-12,33,65,79,117,119,121,197,236
  miraculous and 103
  praise and 100
  -powers 4-7,9,11,13,42,69,123,146,159,188,197,209
  pulsation of 165
  remedial power of 159,160
  shepherd of 167
  and stigmata 144

-task 126
-testimony 93
-tides 185
-tone 138
and true creation 123
-urgency 207
-will 36
speech 42,92,97,221
Spheres of Light 50
spiritual
    atoms 3,7,46
    practices 3,9
    Presences 18
    Worlds 25,40,41,43,46,148
stewardship 6,48,61,65,72,82,85,171,215,219,223,240
subconscious
    mind 10
    world 10,11
symbols 12,44,45

T

talents 9,34,36,48,49,57,58,69,71,82,126,197,221,232,240
teacher (teaching) 16,71,75,89
telepathy 11,12,41-43,186,187,242
tenderness 2,57,93,179
Third
    Heaven 50
    vitality 199,218,251
tithe 244
tribal genesis 227
truth 53,75,120,122,128,137,161,162,179,193,208,221,
    230,251

V

vibration 7
vibratory hum 7-11,33,99,117,119,157,236
vortice pool 245

W

wisdom 23,59,68,69,75,84,89,105,131,161,162,179,231
Word of God 71,247,249
World of God 70,95,134
    of Light 178
worship 54,57,149,243-245,248

BOOKS AND LESSONS
by Ann Ree Colton

BOOKS

WATCH YOUR DREAMS
An invaluable and necessary book revealing the soul-codes in dreams and their symbols.

ETHICAL E S P
An important book defining the difference between lower and higher ESP

THE JESUS STORY
A miracle book in timing to the need for miracles.

THE HUMAN SPIRIT
A scientific, spiritual, and healing book on the creation, purpose and destiny of man.

PROPHET FOR THE ARCHANGELS
The life story of Ann Ree Colton.

THE SOUL AND THE ETHIC
A profound book on the soul and on the etheical use of soul power.

THE KING
From the personal, hieroglyphic journal of Ann Ree Colton.

DRAUGHTS OF REMEMBRANCE
An extraordinary book on the subject of reincarnation.

MEN IN WHITE APPAREL
A book of vital revelations about death and the life after death.

THE VENERABLE ONE
An initiatory book for those who love Nature and who would unveil Nature's secrets.

VISION FOR THE FUTURE
A prophetic book to comfort men in a perilous time.

THE LIVELY ORACLES
A prophetic book on world events.

ISLANDS OF LIGHT
A book of initiation with an underlying prophetic theme.

PRECEPTS FOR THE YOUNG
Appreciated by the adult . . . inspiring to the child . . . and beneficial to the family.

MONTHLY LESSONS

Personalized home-study lessons. Complete philosophical, practical and spiritual instruction.

ARC PUBLISHING CO.

P.O. Box 1138   Glendale, California 91209